AF378722

Pieter Verheyde

CHAMPAGNE

A sparkling discovery

PHOTOGRAPHY
Andrew Verschetze

LANNOO

CHAMPAGNE, A SPECIAL MOMENT

Of course, champagne belongs at parties, weddings and births, victories, diplomas, inaugurations and promotions. What we sometimes forget about this sparkling pleasure is that champagne is also wine, wine with a very special status. Each champagne has its own character, its style, its moment and its taste. We speak of brut and sec, of white and rosé, but the nuances are infinitely greater, as every champagne lover will testify. What also makes champagne special is that there is no other wine where human knowledge and skills play such an important role. Nowhere is so much time spent on the whole process, from tending the vine to the final product, the bottle with its special cork and wire hood.

Together with Burgundy and Piedmont, Champagne is one of my favourite wine regions. I travel there again and again to taste, but also to hear stories. What's this family's history? What technique have they developed here? Why do these plots give such a special grape? I am happy to take my readers with me on these trips, because the more you know about a wine and its maker, the greater the pleasure you have in drinking it.

In the last thirty or forty years, a lot has changed in Champagne. There have been many new *récoltants-manipulants*, sons have taken over family estates, new generations have opted for new styles, in some houses veritable revolutions have occurred. At the same time, however, a certain sluggishness reigns in the region. Champagne making takes time and, unlike other wines, it is not marketed after one year. A nice Burgundy is ready after sixteen months, a good champagne needs to ripen.

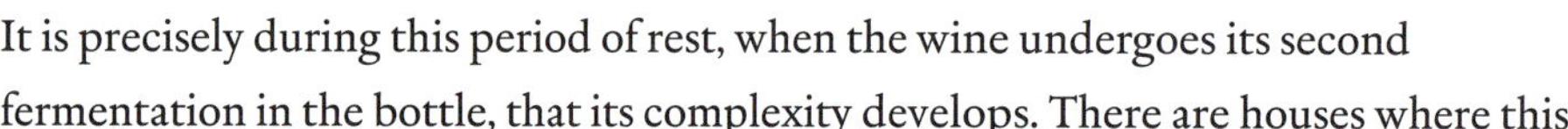

It is precisely during this period of rest, when the wine undergoes its second fermentation in the bottle, that its complexity develops. There are houses where this ripening *sur lattes* lasts seven to ten years, sometimes even longer. In the houses we visited for this book, this is often the case. This book includes world-famous names, but also very modest houses, where the grower welcomes us with mud on his hands. We have selected them based on the precision with which they make their wines and on the emotion that these summon. Because pleasure and emotion is what champagne is all about. When I taste a really delicious wine, I get chills up my left arm. Then it's no longer about notes in a tasting book, but all about delicious or not. In a world where everything goes fast, experience is important, and when such a moment of respite occurs, you really need to enjoy it.

In my childhood days, champagne was a celebration, but above all an exclusive product, a sign of social status. The wine itself was subordinate; the most important thing was that there were bubbles in it. Today, I note that passionate winegrowers almost want to get rid of the bubbles, to display better the beauty of the wine itself.

Of course, trends are also involved. Today, extra brut and brut nature are the most sought after champagnes, while formerly demi-sec was popular. In those days, champagne was not drunk as an aperitif, but as a dessert wine. Meanwhile, the function of the festive drink – the bubbles at a birth – is increasingly taken over by cava, while the true enthusiasts are looking for special champagnes made with passion and love. Increasingly, the grape growers are working ecologically, realizing the need to respect their soils and keep them healthy. A delicious final product calls for healthy grapes from healthy soil.

The majority of smaller producers whom we discuss here are people who work plot by plot. Everywhere it is the same story: the work in the vineyard, good grapes and very precise pressing are a large part of the art. Then time, lots of time, which for producers also means that they must be financially strong. In the thousands of bottles that sleep in the cellars, it is also their capital that is sleeping. You really feel small when you stand next to cuvées whose content will come onto the market only in 2030.

These people are building the future. Which in many cases also begs the question of succession. What if the children are not interested in continuing the estate?

For us, consumers and sommeliers, there is just the pleasure of the tasting and the fun of the moment. Champagne is something you drink at a party, when meeting with friends, in the afternoon at times, a moment of relaxation after effort... or to do

something good. I will never open a bottle thoughtlessly: a nice champagne demands respect, especially if you know the road it has travelled. Personally, I detest wine snobs. Wine is made for drinking together, for sharing pleasure. Even when you taste in a circle of friends, it has to remain relaxed.

There are people who play sports to relieve the pressure, and there are those who open a good bottle. I belong to the second category.

Pieter Verheyde

CONTENT

CHAMPAGNE J. DE TELMONT

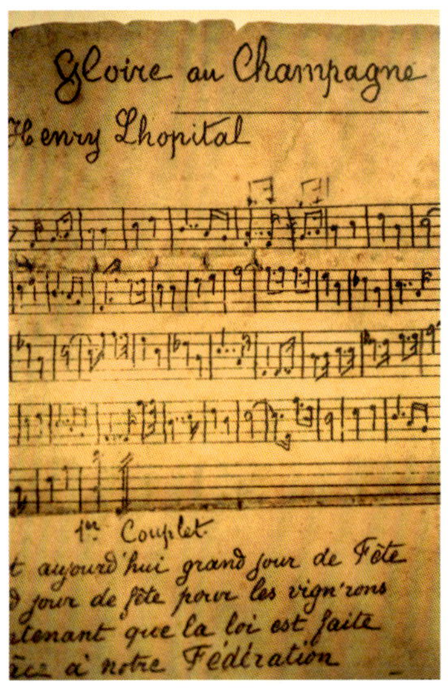

In 1911, the phylloxera insect did great damage in the Champagne region. Entire vineyards were destroyed, leaving hardly any grapes with which to produce wine. New plantings were needed, but that required time. Swindlers purchased grapes from other wine regions and even used other products to produce champagne. For the grape growers this was a catastrophe, and they made clear their unhappiness at this course of action. A revolt smouldered in the villages of Damery and Venteuil.

Only in 1927 was a law promulgated requiring all champagne houses to use only grapes picked within the specified area. Thus originated the Champagne appellation, which is the most rigorous in the world.

The history of the Maison J. de Telmont began in these troubled times, with Henri Lhopital, the first of his generation. Innovative and resourceful, he decided early on not just to grow grapes, but also to process them himself: from 1912 on, he sells his Champagne under his own name.

Eventually, his son André succeeded him. With his knowledge of the terroir and selling techniques, André collected grapes from the best plots of the region. That gave him the opportunity to produce high quality champagne.

Négociant manipulant

650,000 bottles

Champagne J. de Telmont

1, avenue de Champagne

F–51480 DAMERY

+33 3 26 58 40 33

www.champagne-de-telmont.com

André Lhopital went looking for a name that was better suited to the prestige of his *cuvées* than his own family name. One of the plots from which the grapes came was called 'Les Beaumonts' but he could not sell his champagne under this name, so André decided to modify it. In 1949, the Maison de Champagne J. de Telmont was born.

André Lhopital's son Serge brings us to the third generation. Serge had vast production knowledge and commercial talent, boosting sales even further. Year after year, harvest after harvest, the champagne gained recognition and even a certain authority. It was Serge who established J. de Telmont at its current address, where in 1968 new cellars were installed.

←
Nec pluribus impar is Latin for 'Not unequal to many'. The house motto but also a reference to the device of 'Sun King' Louis XIV.

↖
A *foudre* at J. de Telmont

↓
Champagne maturing *sur lattes*

→
The traditional way of attaching the string to the cork

Today, his son Bertrand and daughter Pascale continue the business as the fourth generation. Brother and sister complement each other well. The passing on of knowledge of the terroir and production methods are values that the company continues to cherish. The champagne is still stored corked. Part of the vinification is done in large 50-hectolitre *foudres* (upright barrels), which gives the wines complexity and *matière*.

The many years of experience in both vineyard cellar and the hours spent on the bottles make J. de Telmont one of the great champagnes.

The J. de Telmont house is strongly in favour of allowing the champagne to age for longer than is usually done, that is at least three years *sur lattes* (on racks) for the *bruts* and more than six years for the millésimés. This process yields greater complexity and finer bubbles. This, of course, requires patience, but with this vision this house wants to distinguish itself at world level from other sparkling wines and bring an even higher quality champagne to the market.

The vineyard today covers 33 hectares and has eight crus planted with the three grapes, Pinot Noir, Pinot Meunier and Chardonnay. The vineyards are spread across the villages of Cumières, Damery, Fleury-La-Rivière and Romery.

J. de Telmont has a total production of 650,000 bottles, representing from 63 hectares of 40 different crus, Grands, Premiers as well as other crus. This accounts for the great diversity in the Maison's cuvées.

CUVÉES AND MILLÉSIMÉS

THE CLASSICS

GRANDE RÉSERVE BRUT

assembly	assembly of Pinot Noir, Pinot Meunier and Chardonnay
type	brut
production	36 months in the cellar
results	suppleness and freshness

GRAND ROSÉ BRUT

assembly	assembly of 85% Chardonnay and 15% Pinot Noir and Pinot Meunier
type	brut
results	elegant, sophisticated, fruity and delicate

THE MILLÉSIMÉS

GRAND VINTAGE (MILLÉSIME 2005)

assembly	40% Pinot Meunier, 40% Chardonnay and 20% Pinot Noir
type	brut
production	vinification and long maturation in stainless steel *cuves*

GRAND BLANC DE BLANCS (MILLÉSIME 2009)

assembly	assembly of different crus of 100% Chardonnay from a single year
type	brut
production	no malolactic fermentation

THE PRESTIGE CUVÉES

CUVÉE OR 1735

This intriguing name refers to the year 1735, in which Louis XV gave permission by *Ordonnance Royale* to commercialize Champagne for the first time in bottles, previously permitted only in barrels. The bottles were sealed with a cork, held together by a hemp string and a lacquer seal.

terroir	the plots are in Chouilly and Avize, in the grand cru region
grape varieties	100% Chardonnay
assembly	millésimé
results	Cuvée OR 2004 is the Maison's *cuvée de Prestige*.

LE GRAND COURONNEMENT

grape varieties	100% Chardonnay
assembly	millésimé 2002

LES ORIGINALES

Concerned with their environment and the preservation of their terroir, the J. de Telmont house started with biodynamic winegrowing on 10 hectares.

CUVÉE 'SANS SOUFRE AJOUTÉ' (WITHOUT ADDED SULPHUR)

production	biodynamic wine-growing

CUVÉE LÉGER DOSAGE

results	The 'LD' (*léger dosage* – light sugar dosage) is a Blanc de Blancs, extra brut and very mineral.

THE HERITAGES COLLECTION

This range is also called the *Vinothèque*, where you will find champagnes of older years, such as the 1969 champagne as well as those of '75, '76, '85, '86, '90, '92 and '95.

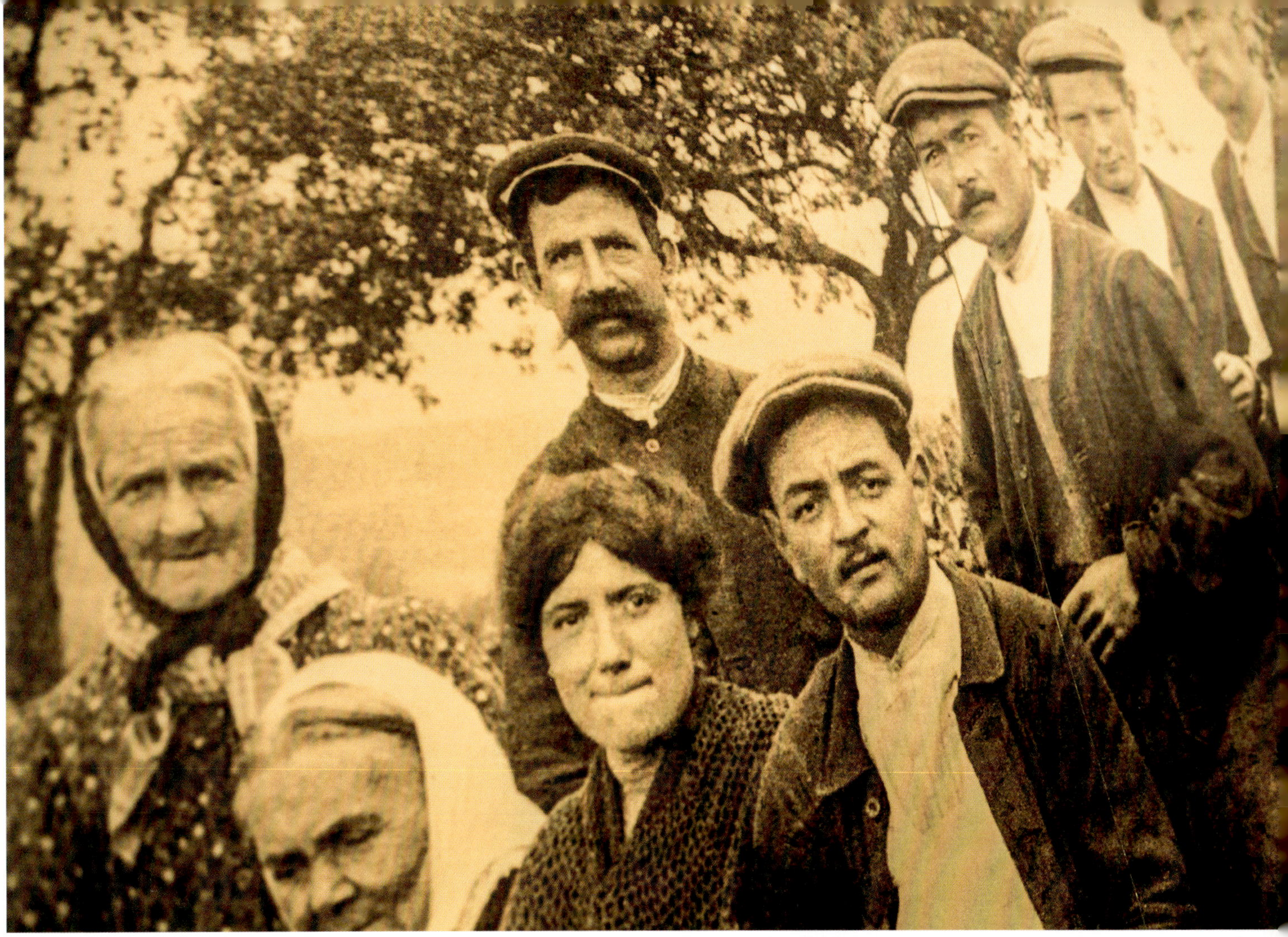

J. DE TELMONT

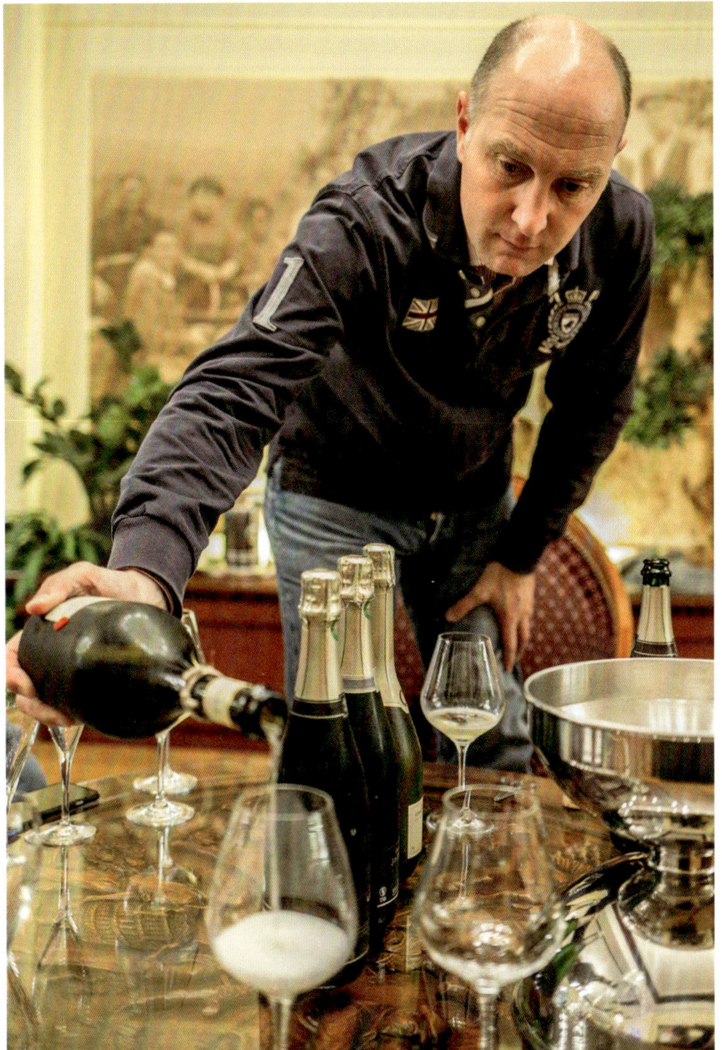

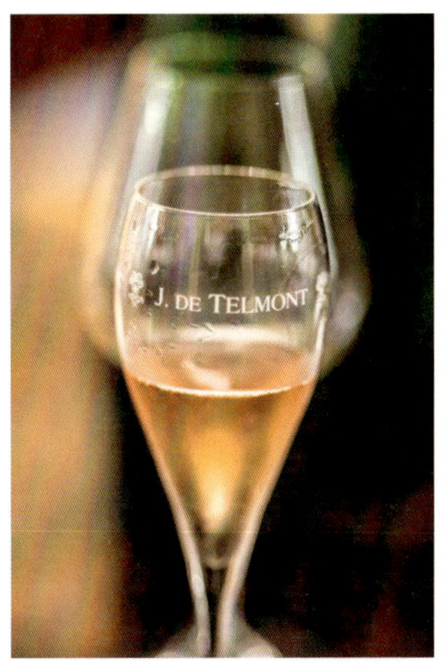

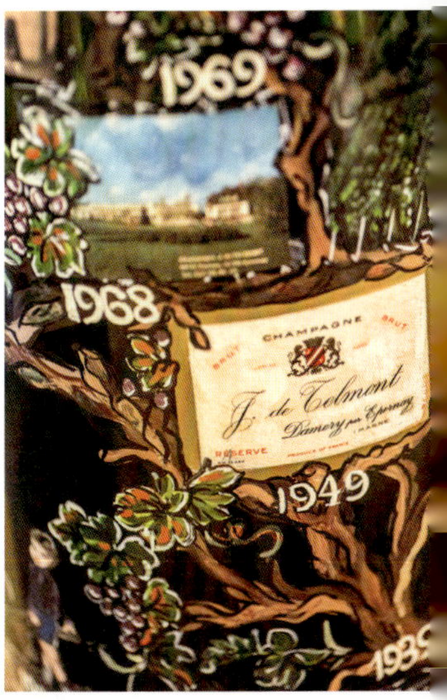
1969
1968
CHAMPAGNE
J. de Telmont
1949

H.L.M

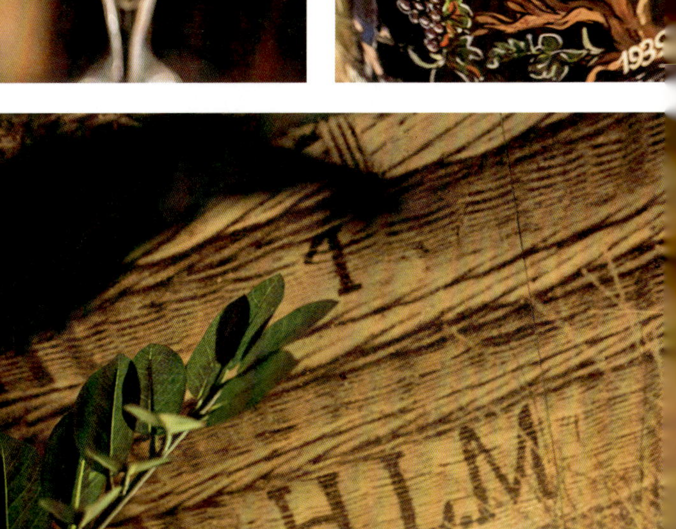

CHAMPAGNE AGRAPART

Pascal Agrapart

In Avize, in the 'Côte des Blancs' region, we meet Pascal Agrapart, owner of
the Agrapart house. For four generations the family has made wine as a *récoltant-manipulant*, and does not buy in grapes.

Pascal is a cool man, very focused and clearly knows what he is doing. Like the
other champagne houses, Agrapart has also had its ups and downs. War and economic
crisis meant that it was not always possible for them to live from their product, and in
hard times their predecessors sold their grapes to *négociants*. Over the years and with
the present generation they have gained more room to move and ensure stability.

After completing his military service in 1981, Pascal acquired the necessary
knowledge in Bordeaux. When he returned to Champagne, most houses were in the
habit of working with pesticides and herbicides. Pascal refused and decided to go
back to roots. Everyone declared him crazy. He set to work, plot by plot, tended the
vineyard meticulously and reduced the yield per hectare. Today,
as a result, he has twelve persons in his employ, one per hectare.
Champagne is the region in France with a high density of grape
vines per hectare, around 9,000 vines per hectare. This is also laid
down by law.

Récoltant manipulant

100,000 bottles

Champagne Agrapart

57, avenue Jean Jaurès

F–51190 AVIZE

+ 33 3 26 57 51 38

www.champagne-agrapart.com

The Agrapart vineyard comprises about twelve hectares, of which nine hectares of Chardonnay grand cru in Avize, Oger, Cramant and Oiry; two hectares of Chardonnay premier cru in Avenay-Val-d'Or, Bergères-lès-Vertus and Mardeuil; and one hectare of Pinot Noir in Avenay-Val-d'Or, premier cru in Montagne de Reims.

This gives a total of 750 hectolitres, accounting for 100,000 bottles a year. Of these, 35% are for the French market and 65% for export.

Agrapart is a biological winemaker. This means living and working in the vineyard form a single whole. The soil, the health of the vines and the authentic expression that the grapes get from terroir are first priority at Agrapart.

Agrapart owns more than seventy plots of 8,000 vines per hectare, with a 41B rootstock. The old vines are an inheritance from his father, Pierre Agrapart, who chose the vines by so-called *sélection massive*, whereby the best vines are selected and allowed to grow.

With his great love for Burgundy, Pascal uses the chablis pruning method. This means that he takes into account the problems of the estate, shows respect for sap flow and controls foliage growth. Ten bunches of one hundred grams each are better than five bunches of two hundred grams.

The vines are trained by hand to allow sun and wind to do their work, which is the best way to combat disease. To stimulate plant resistance, Pascal uses compost. He also uses copper and sulphur treatments, tailored to the presence of parasites and climatic conditions. The compost is prepared with local ingredients in spring and in autumn, and fed to the plant together with the compost of compost biologist Timothy Bolander.

To promote root depth, mechanical degrassing is used to remove weeds and superficial roots.

Vinification is done only with top grapes, manually and selectively in small basins. Agrapart has two classic vertical 4,000 kg Coquard presses that give high-quality pressing.

The wine has a natural sediment without the addition of enzymes. There is little to no chapitalization. The alcoholic fermentation with natural yeast cells occurs in vats or in large 600-litre barrels, the so-called *demi-muids*. The complete malolactic fermentation is produced by the temperature in the cellar. By passing cold air in winter, the tartaric acid precipitates into crystals, producing tartaric acid stabilization.

The wine then lies for six months *sur lies* without collage or filtration, because for Agrapart every treatment weakens the original message. In spring, the wine is bottled and stored at a constant temperature in the basement.

← Fermentation takes place in temperature-regulated stainless steel tanks.

Conclusion   Respect for the terroir, the soil and the living underground that is cultivated by man is paramount at Agrapart.

The vineyard is worked with respect for nature, with the wine ripening to the rhythm of the seasons in the cellars.

↓ Attractive personalized cork caps

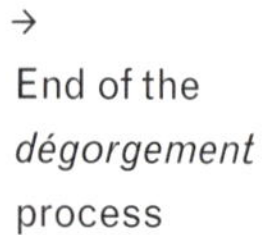

→
End of the
dégorgement
process

→
Bottles are carefully
checked before being
placed in the freezer
ahead of *dégorgement*.

↓
Freezing the bottle
neck *sur pointe*

CUVÉES AND MILLÉSIMÉS

Agrapart has a first "gourmand" or greedy wine, the 7 Crus Brut.

The Terroirs cuvée is an assembly wine.

This house has a great preference for *parcelle* wines, which means that the wine

takes its identity from the plot (*parcelle*), making it possible to produce a millésimé

every year. There are three millésimé monocrus, Minéral, Avizoise and Venus.

These are genuine champagnes with the Agrapart signature.

7 Crus – Premier Vin

terroir	This is an assembly of seven crus: Avize, Oger, Cramant, Oiry, Avenay-Val-d'Or, Bergères-lès-Vertus and Madeuil.
grape varieties	10% Pinot Noir, 90% Chardonnay
assembly	The champagne consists of 60% wine of the most recent year and 40% of the year before. These are mostly grand cru réserve wines, half of which have been stored in large 600-litre barrels (*demi-muids*).
type	brut

Terroirs – Blanc de Blancs Grand Cru

classification	grand cru
terroir	an assembly of the main cuvées Avize, Oger, Cramant and Oiry
grape varieties	100% Chardonnay
assembly	The champagne consists of 40% wine of the most recent year and 60% of the year before.
type	extra brut

Minéral Blanc de Blancs Grand Cru

classification	grand cru
terroir	an assembly of the main cuvées of Les Champboutons in Avize and Les Bionnes in Cramant
soil	Dominated by lime. The cuvées have a similar geological profile, namely a limestone-rich but poor soil.
grape varieties	100% Chardonnay. The vines for this champagne are over 50 years old.
assembly	millésimé
type	extra brut
results	tension and minerality

Minéral Collection Blanc de Blancs Grand Cru

classification	grand cru
terroir	the same assembly as the Minéral Blanc de Blancs Grand Cru
grape varieties	100% Chardonnay
assembly	millésimé
type	extra brut

Avizoise Blanc de Blancs Grand Cru

classification	grand cru
terroir	Assembly of the main cuvées from Les Robards and Gros Yeux in Avize. The vineyard is located on a high south-southeast-facing slope. This is another Avize style. The vines are over 60 years old and hence the oldest of the estate, but on the best slopes.
soil	dominated by clay
grape varieties	100% Chardonnay
assembly	millésimé
type	extra brut
results	matter and richness

VÉNUS BLANC DE BLANCS
GRAND CRU MILLÉSIMÉ – BRUT NATURE

classification	grand cru
terroir	Assembly from vines from the 60 acres of La Fosse in Avize. This vineyard, planted in 1959, uses no heavy machinery. The plot is sloping and is worked only by man and horse, another aspect of Avize.
soil	lime on top of clay
grape varieties	100% Chardonnay
assembly	millésimé
type	brut nature

EXPÉRIENCE BLANC DE BLANCS GRAND CRU

classification	grand cru
terroir	assembly of main cuvées of old vines from Les Robards and Les Bionnes in Avize.
grape varieties	100% Chardonnay
type	brut nature
production	The idea is to deliver a 100% pure product. The alcoholic strength is natural and there is no chaptalization. The first fermentation is natural. For the *prise de mousse*, the must (grape juice) from the following harvest is used to add the equivalent of 24g of sugar and yeast. Own yeast and own sugar ... Here we have no millésimé.
results	Expérience is a successful experiment.

COMPLANTÉE GRAND CRU

classification	grand cru
terroir	These are different grape varieties planted on the same terroir. As a result, the grape variety is secondary to the terroir. *Complantée* or co-planting means planting different grape varieties on the same plot. In this case, these are Chardonnay, Pinot Noir, Pinot Meunier, Pinot Blanc, Arbane and Petit Meslier. The young vines were planted in 2003 on 30 acres in La Fosse à Bull. Co-plantation is intended to show that the terroir dominates the grape variety. Today we cannot really perceive the different grape properties, so this is probably the terroir effect.
grape varieties	Pinot Noir, Pinot Meunier, Chardonnay, Arbane, Petit Meslier, Pinot Blanc
type	extra brut

Champagne Agrapart

←
View of the
grand cru vineyard

→
Wood prunings

HAMPAGNE
CART-SALMON
ison Fondée en 1818

CHAMPAGNE BILLECART-SALMON

François and Antoine Roland-Billecart:
'Privilégier la qualité et viser l'excellence'
(Prioritizing quality and being vigilant for excellence.)

Back in 1818, Nicolas François Billecart married Élisabeth Salmon. This marriage marked the birth of the champagne house Billecart-Salmon. The newlyweds were both residents of Mareuil-sur-Aÿ, where the champagne house still exists today. Nicolas François' grandfather had already produced wine in the 17th century and received permission from Louis XIV to use his own coat of arms. Billecart-Salmon is located alongside the Marne canal and within walking distance of Philipponnat, another champagne house.

In 2018, Billecart-Salmon celebrates its 200th anniversary. Inside the champagne house, every family member has their own special task. This works very well, as the business is already in the sixth generation.

On arriving at the domain, we are overwhelmed by the beautiful garden, which is tended with great care. For the family, the garden remains the big eye-catcher.

Négociant manipulant
2,000,000 bottles

Champagne Billecart-Salmon
40, rue Carnot
F–51160 MAREUIL-SUR-AŸ
+33 3 26 52 60 22
www.champagne-billecart.fr

We are welcomed by François Roland-Billecart, who heads up the estate, accompanied by Jean Roland-Billecart, François Domi, *chef de cave*, Denis Blée, vineyard manager and Alexandre Bader, general manager and responsible for the image of the champagne house.

'Champagne is our life', François Roland-Billecart tells us: 'We were born with it. We've all grown up here, it's in our genes.' Even the annual vacations to the south don't change this. Champagne is their terroir, their home, their life.

Just after the Second World War, the house was better known for its demi-sec champagnes. This kind of champagne obscured the excess acidity of the aromatic base wine. 'But over the years, we have evolved from a dessert to an aperitif champagne and are now fully devoted to luxury aperitif champagnes.'

At Billecart-Salmon they produce a controlled champagne with lots of finesse. For this, innovative methods are used. For example, vinification is done by cold stabilization, a technique taken over from their brewer grandfather. Cold vinification means that the must is cooled down to 50°C for a few days before fermentation sets in. Alcoholic fermentation lasts for three weeks at a temperature of 12°C. *Chef de cave* François Domi has been making this harmonious and elegant champagne for thirty years: 'In the final fermentation we use less yeast, which gives it a finer sparkle, but this is the choice of the house, it's our house style. Avoiding oxidation problems is one of our hobbyhorses.'

François leads us around and we stop in front of a huge assembly tank, of a size we have never seen at other houses. Precisely how big, we are not told, but the tank is incredibly large. In total, the house uses 450 different barrels in the *cuverie*, along with the big tank. Equally impressive is the stainless steel conveyor belt that transports bottles individually from one floor to another in the three and a half kilometres of cellars.

    Champagne Billecart-Salmon

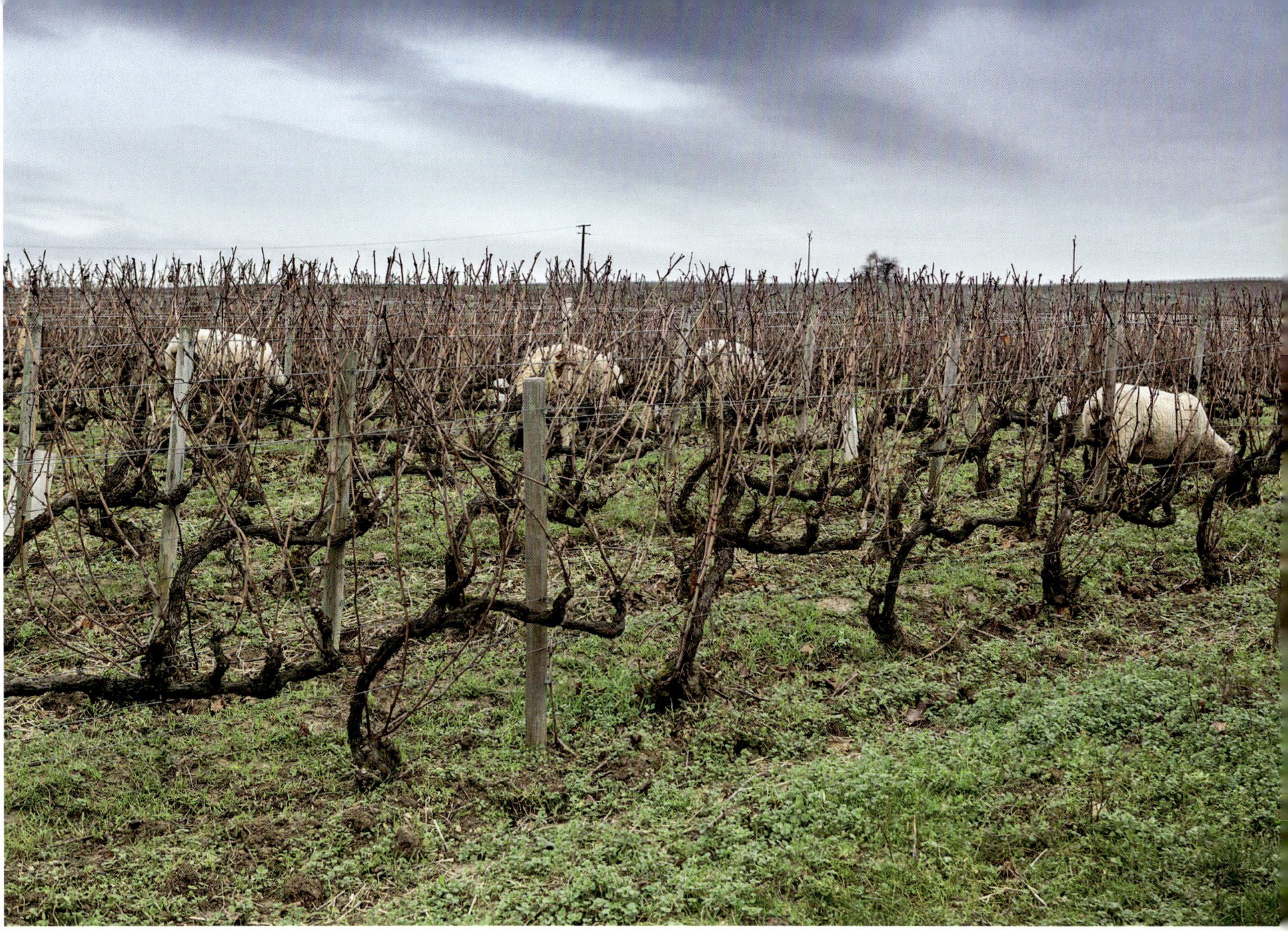

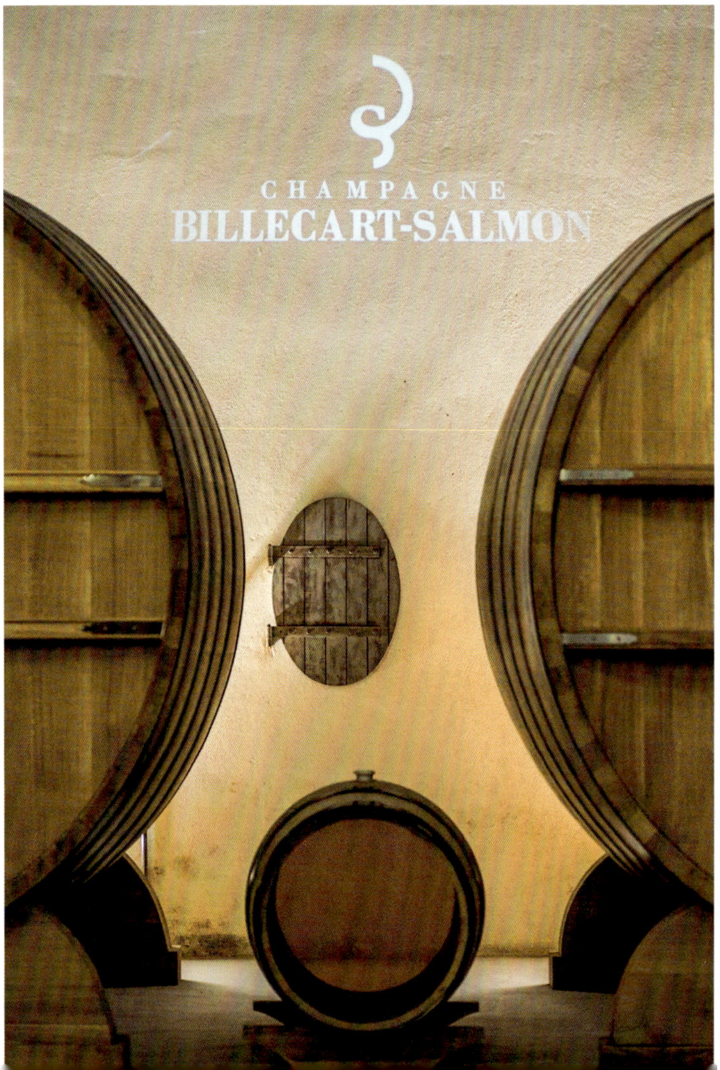
CHAMPAGNE
BILLECART-SALMON

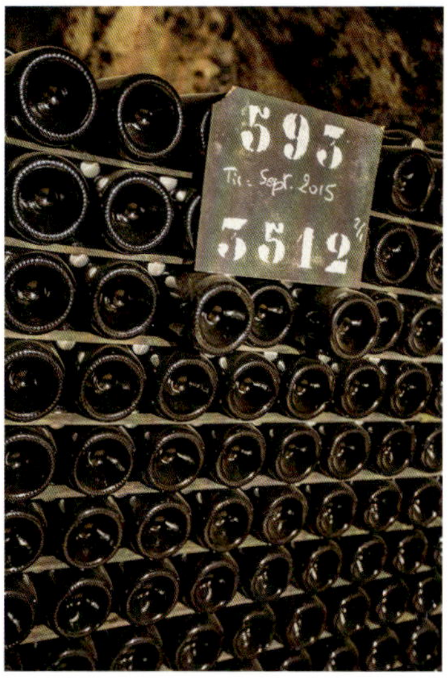
593
3512

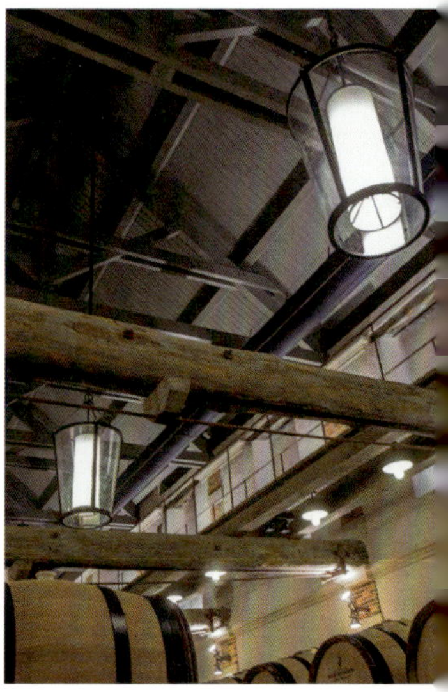

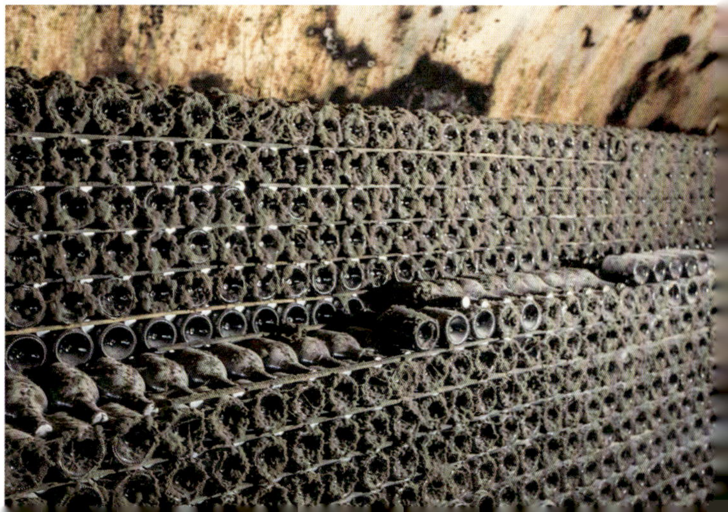

574
P= 10/11
1373
574
10/11

Billecart-Salmon describes itself as a 'small to medium-sized *négociant*'. The house is 95% *négociant* and owns 100 hectares of property. In addition, the house has contracts with the best winegrowers of Avize, Cramant and Le Mesnil-sur-Oger.

<table><tr><td>Conclusion</td><td>

For us, the Clos Saint-Hilaire (Blanc de Noirs brut) is the most excellent champagne. Also especially delicious are the Élisabeth Salmon and the Blanc de Blancs.

We close with François Roland-Billecart's words: 'We are pure business people and have been able to make far-reaching changes, bringing us to a total of 2 million bottles a year. We consider ourselves a medium-sized champagne house, somewhere between mass production and a small family business.'

</td></tr></table>

←
Pupitre bottle rack in the cellar carved into the chalk

↙
A nice example of 'Cladosporium' a genus of fungi appearing during storage

CUVÉES AND MILLÉSIMÉS

CUVÉES

Brut Rosé,
BOTTLED IN THE WORLD-FAMOUS BOTTLE

grape varieties	Pinot Noir, Pinot Meunier, Chardonnay
type	brut
assembly	an assembly of Chardonnay, Pinot Meunier and Pinot Noir (red vinification)

Brut réserve

terroir	The grapes come only from the best plots of the Marne.
grape varieties	Pinot Noir, Pinot Meunier, Chardonnay From 100-year-old vines
assembly	assembly of three different years
type	brut
results	subtle and harmonious

Blanc de Blancs grand cru

classification	grand cru
terroir	five different crus: Avize, Chouilly, Cramant, Le Mesnil-sur-Oger and Oger
grape varieties	100% Chardonnay
assembly	assembly of two different years

Extra brut

grape varieties	Pinot Noir, Pinot Meunier, Chardonnay
type	extra brut
dosage	0 g/litre
results	pure and natural

Brut sous bois, the newcomer in the story

grape varieties	Pinot Noir, Pinot Meunier, Chardonnay
type	brut
production	vinified in the barrel

Demi-sec

grape varieties	Pinot Noir, Pinot Meunier, Chardonnay
dosage	more sugar added than the Brut Réserve
type	demi-sec

MILLÉSIMÉS

VINTAGE

assembly	millésimé
type	extra brut
results	intense and tempting

BLANC DE BLANCS

assembly	millésimé
results	Elegant Chardonnay of the Côte des Blancs, mineral and precise. In it you find the strength of Avize, the structure and storage qualities of Le Mesnil-sur-Oger, and the freshness and finesse of Cramant and Chouilly.

NICOLAS FRANÇOIS BILLECART

terroir	an assembly of Côte des Blancs from Chouilly and Cramant and of Pinot Noir from the Montagne de Reims
assembly	millésimé
production	This champagne is vinified in traditional barrels.
results	Balanced and rich. This champagne was created in 1964 in memory of the founder of the house. In 1999, the cuvée Nicolas François Billecart 1959 was voted 'Champagne du Millénaire' in Stockholm by a panel of experts in a blind tasting of 150 champagnes from the largest houses. The 1961 millésimé ended in twelfth position.

ÉLISABETH SALMON

assembly	millésimé
type	brut
results	This champagne was created in 1988 in memory of the founder's wife.

CLOS SAINT-HILAIRE, BLANC DE NOIRS

grape varieties	100% Pinot Noir on vines from 1964
assembly	millésimé
type	brut
production	The wine is vinified in small barrels. 1995 was a great year for the vineyard and this was also their first millésimé. One plot is closed off on three sides. It is near the vinification cellar. During the winter, sheep graze in this vineyard, which is unusual.
results	This champagne was developed by François Roland in 1950 and named after the patron saint of the church of Mareuil-sur-Aÿ. It has huge potential.

CHAMPAGNE SAVART

Frédéric Savart, *the enfant terrible*

Frédéric Savart greets us with his favourite quote from Pierre Champsaur: 'Faire ce que tu aimes, c'est la liberté. Aimer ce que tu fais, c'est le bonheur'. *(Doing what you like is freedom. Liking what you do is happiness.)* With such an opener, we immediately know that we have in front of us no common or garden winegrower. Frédéric Savart is the *enfant terrible* among champagne growers. Only on the sixth attempt do we finally get an appointment with him.

Champagne Savart dates back to 1947. Grandfather René gained experience in the Écueil cooperative and collected 700 bottles. Like for many in those difficult days, it was hard to live from champagne. In 1970, his son Daniel took over and the house maintained a small production until the mid-1980s. In 2005, Frédéric became head of the estate under the watchful eye of his father Daniel, who remains very present and receives visitors with Frédéric.

Frédéric was not at all predestined for wine-growing. He was a professional footballer and had signed a contract at the Stade de Reims. Unfortunately, a serious injury put an end to his career. Nor did his studies go as well as could be desired. At the time, however, he met his present wife. Father Daniel asked his son to return home, hoping he could persuade him to grow champagne. Frédéric was 20 years old, not even knowing what alcohol tasted like.

In Avize he gained his baccalauréat school-leaving certificate. During that time, he got to know Anselme Selosse's cousin and two other champagne students, one a member of the Krug staff and the other a student of the Bollinger house. They hit it off and for a year talked together about wine and barriques. At one point, Anselme Selosse's cousin invited Frédéric to the family estate. Selosse told him of his preference for wine from the barrel. For Frédéric, it sounded like messages from another planet (Selosse was then still totally unknown).

Champagne Savart

1, chemin de Sacy

F–51500 ÉCUEIL

(Montagne de Reims)

+33 3 26 84 91 60

www.champagne-savart.com

51

But he was totally taken by the idea. He informed his father and told him that he wanted to make champagne in the same way. Wines in barrels have more substance and are fuller in taste. Father Daniel allowed Frédéric to carry out some tests on different plots – it was now 2003-2004. Daniel was forced to humbly admit that his son made sublime champagne and encouraged him to follow his own style completely. From 2003-2004, the Savart house was built up again from scratch.

The Savart vineyards are spread over two villages, Écueil (Montagne de Reims) and Villers-aux-Noeuds. The house produces four hectares of grapes, three at Écueil and one at Villers-aux-Noeuds (le Mont Benoît).

Frédéric ferments all his champagnes in the barrel, but what surprises us most is that we cannot perceive whatsoever any expression of wood. Wood is used mainly as an oxygen regulator but not for the taste. Barrel fermentation ensures that the champagne is energy-rich and vibrant.

↑
View over the 'La Petite Montagne' vineyard

↗
A moment to look forward to: the *habillage* or corking of the bottle

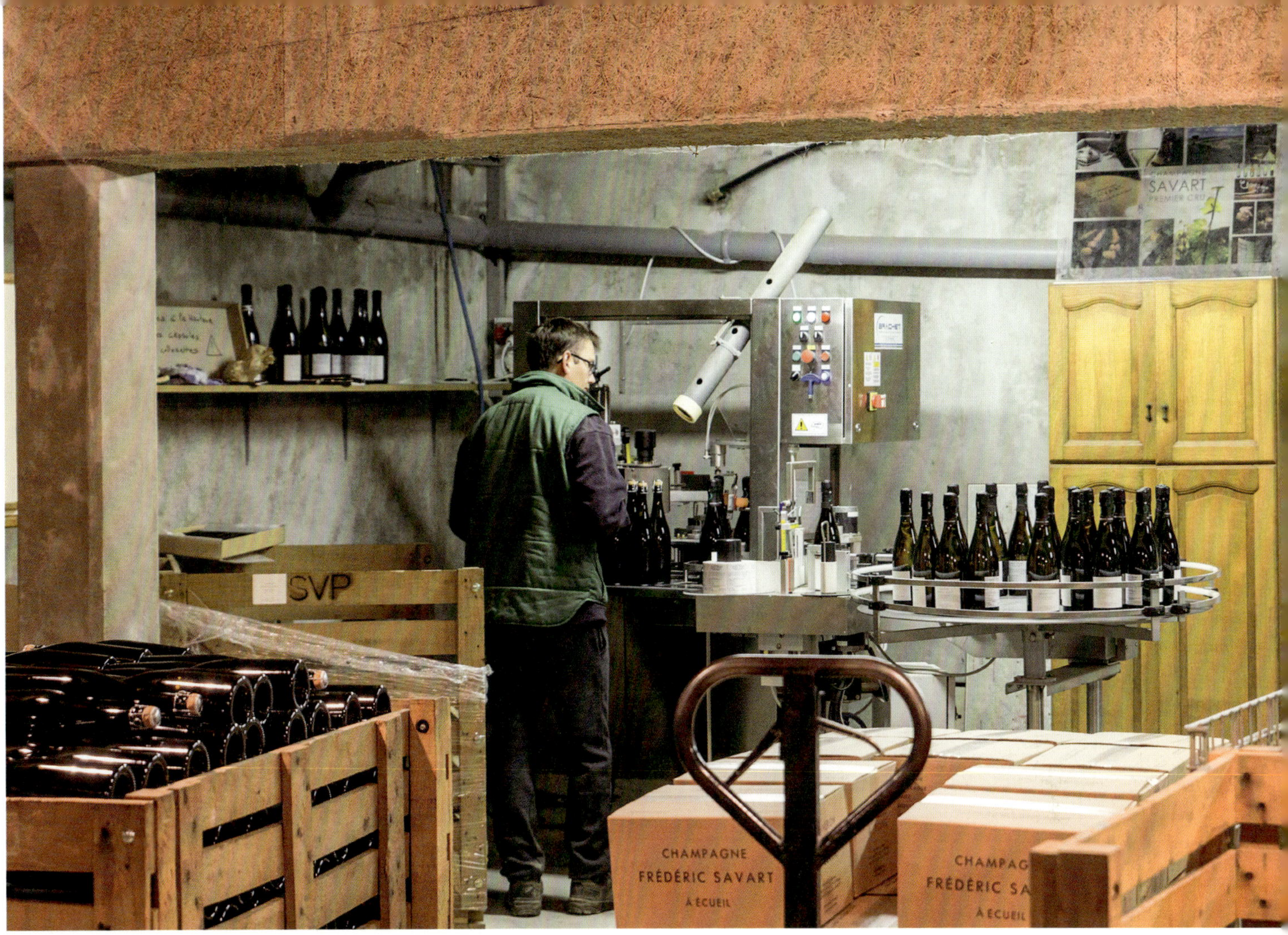
SAVART
PREMIER CRU
SVP
CHAMPAGNE
FRÉDÉRIC SAVART
À ECUEIL

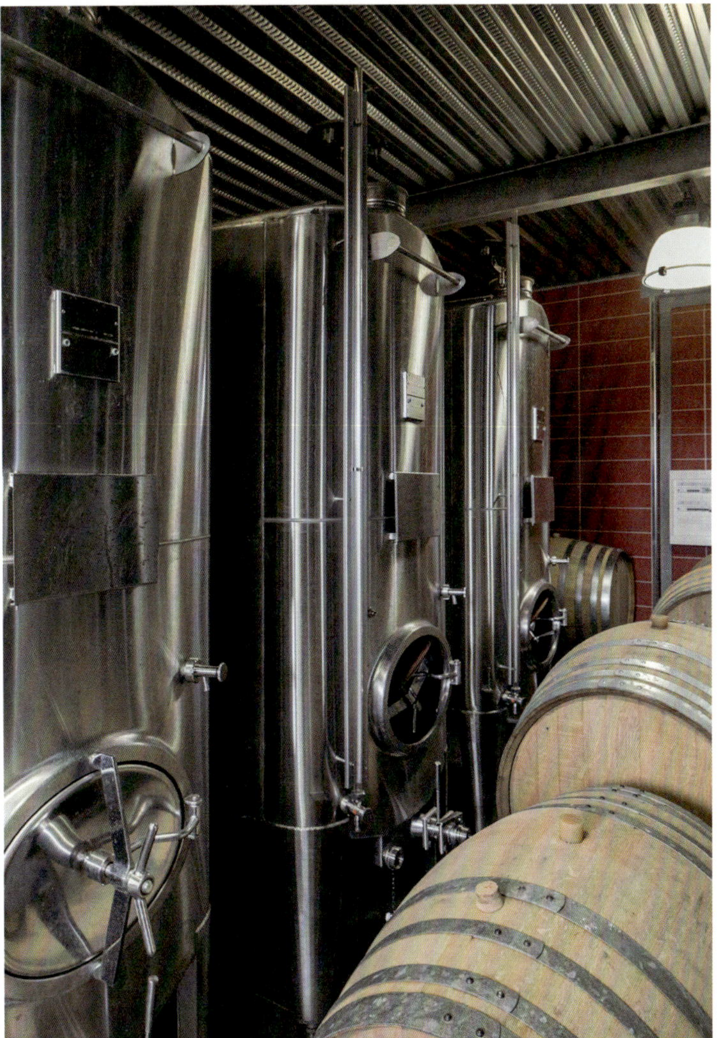

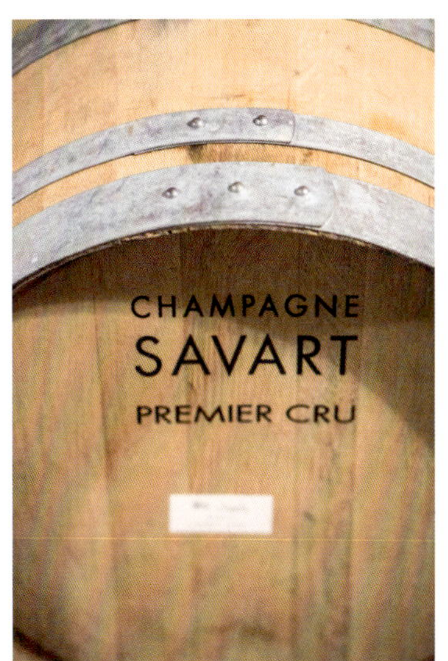

CHAMPAGNE
SAVART
PREMIER CRU

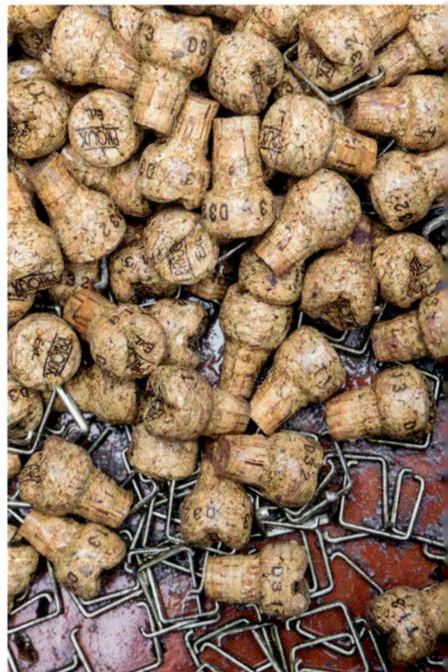

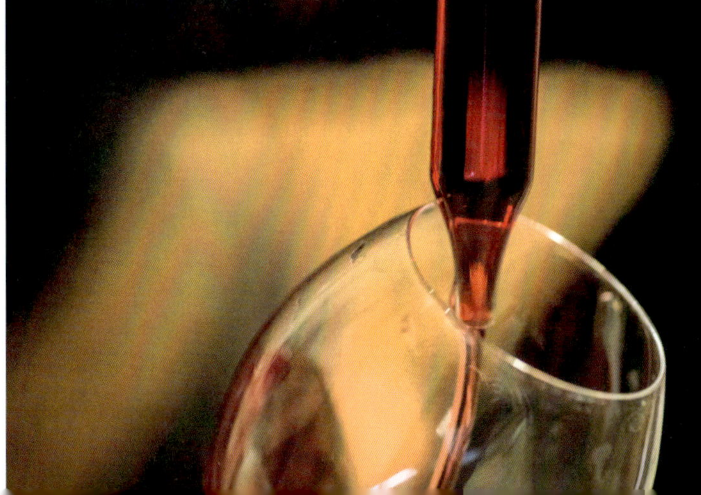

Frédéric uses barrels from Burgundy, especially from Meursault, and wooden
barrels from the forests near Écueil. 95% of the vinification takes place in Austrian
'Stockinger' barrels, which are very popular with winemakers.

Making Champagne is not complicated for Frédéric. For him, everything is
about having the best grapes, barrels and alcoholic fermentation. As a member of
'Les Artisans de Champagne' he follows the philosophy of using as little sulphite as
possible, with no malolactic processing and no *bâtonnage*. Frédéric's trademark is
keeping everything as natural as possible and keeping the acidity in the wine.

He calls his champagnes 'vins identitaires', unique wines, far from standardized
flavours. Frédéric himself is a great wine lover and does not shy from drinking wines
from various other estates. He likes visiting restaurants and prefers to taste his wines
blindfolded. According to Frédéric, in this way he gets to know the people behind
the wine in front of him.

The Savart champagnes are unfortunately not known to the general public.
They are very rare, but extremely popular with the wine connoisseurs among us.

The Savart house produces 30,000 to 40,000 bottles a year, of which 65% for export
to, among others, the USA, Canada, Finland, Norway, Sweden, Belgium,
the Netherlands and Russia. This requires a lot of logistics.

↓
Frédéric Savart,
ex-football
player and *enfant
terrible* in action
during tasting

Conclusion

Champagne Savart made a strong impression on us. The wine really has its own
identity, in which you can clearly recognize its creator's inventiveness. Frédéric is
very closely involved in the whole process, which, together with the technology
and expertise, all serves the emotion, the feeling you experience when drinking his
champagne.

For us, this is a real top house and a must-have in the cellar.

This champagne is rare, yet still affordable.

CUVÉES AND MILLÉSIMÉS

Le Mont Benoît

classification	premier cru
terroir	Villers-aux-Nœuds
soil	clay, limestone
grape varieties	95% Pinot Noir, 5% Chardonnay
dosage	3 g/litre
type	extra brut

Expression

classification	premier cru
terroir	Écueil
soil	clay, limestone
grape varieties	100% Pinot Noir, very old vines
dosage	3 g/litre
type	brut nature
production	10 months *sur lies*

L'Ouverture

classification	premier cru
terroir	Écueil
grape varieties	100% Pinot Noir
assembly	millésimé
dosage	7 g/litre
type	brut

Bulle de rosé

classification	premier cru
terroir	Écueil
grape varieties	70% Pinot Noir, 22% Chardonnay, 8% Pinot Noir in red wine
dosage	6 g/litre
type	brut

Millésime 2013

terroir	Écueil, Villers-aux-Nœuds, Hamlets of Les Rosets and Mont Benoît
grape varieties	60% Pinot Noir, 40% Chardonnay
assembly	millésimé
dosage	3 g/litre
type	extra brut

Expression rosé

classification	premier cru
terroir	Écueil
soil	clay, limestone
grape varieties	100% Pinot Noir, old vines
assembly	millésimé
dosage	0 g/litre
type	brut nature
production	10 months *sur lies*

Le Mont Benoît (millésimé)

classification	premier cru
terroir	Villers-aux-Nœuds
soil	clay, limestone
grape varieties	95% Pinot Noir, 5% Chardonnay
assembly	millésimé
dosage	3 g/litre

Le Mont des Chrétiens

classification	premier cru
terroir	Écueil
grape varieties	100% Chardonnay
assembly	millésimé
dosage	3 g/litre
type	extra brut

L'accomplie

classification	premier cru
terroir	Écueil, Villers-aux-Nœuds
grape varieties	80% Pinot Noir, 20% Chardonnay
dosage	5 g/litre
type	extra brut

CHAMPAGNE ULYSSE COLLIN

**Olivier Collin,
passion for the parcel**

The estate Ulysse Collin is situated in the winegrowing community of Congy along the Morin slopes, a few kilometres southwest of the Côte des Blancs. At first sight, Olivier looks more like an artist than a champagn maker.

The Collin family has grown grapes since 1812, but Olivier's career has not followed a straight path. He studied law and discovered a passion for the great Bourgogne wines and a desire to produce champagne himself.

Before taking over the vineyards and expanding his knowledge, Olivier interned at Anselme Selosse, while at the same time studying viticulture in Bordeaux.

Olivier recuperated the familial estate in March 2003 and began his first year as a winemaker in 2004 on the Pierrieres plot. He decided to focus solely on producing champagnes on separate plots at a time when this type of production generally comprised only a few thousand bottles.

When Olivier took over the company, the soil in his vineyards had not been cultivated for 20 years. His first investment was a tractor to plough the terrain and reactivate the microbiological life so vital for the production of great terroir wines. Thus his mode of viticulture was born, pragmatic and responsive to nature in a non-certified agrobiological fashion.

Champagne Ulysse Collin

19-21, rue des Vignerons

F-51270 CONGY

+ 33 3 26 52 46 62

He does not use copper, which protects the grapes against mildew and other fungi. For him, using copper reduces the microbiological activity in the soil. He does not use pesticides or herbicides, only powdered sulphur. The wines are not filtered. To detoxify the soil and to protect it from erosion, he allows grass to grow between the vineyards after harvest.

Olivier Collin makes five different cuvées. They each retain their own identity. The main elements for maintaining this identity are good barrels, spontaneous fermentation with indigenous yeasts, low dosages of sugar and no filtration.

Olivier believes that in the Champagne region, one of the most industrialized regions of France, the work of the winemakers can contribute to putting the region back on the map.

He himself has a traditional press. This press from the 1950s was the first press in Congy. During harvest it is operated by four people for twelve days, eighteen hours a day. This manual pressing gives the wine more tannin and more flavour. The entire production is fermented and stored in barrels. This happens for the majority of wines, but if necessary, new barrels are used to complete storage. Since 2012, Olivier makes use of *foudres* to store the reserve wines.

Conclusion   The domain Ulysse Collin currently produces 50,000 bottles of charismatic plot-based champagne and has become a point of reference for lovers of great champagne.

←
Storage in
wooden barrels
at Collin

↗
Stainless
steel assembly
tank with the
small wooden
barrels in the
foreground

CUVÉES AND MILLÉSIMÉS

LES PIERRIÈRES, BLANC DE BLANCS
(COTEAU DU MORIN)

terroir	Single vineyard. The grapes come from a 1.2 hectare plot, with little sunlight and a flush chalk layer. The slope faces south-south-east.
soil	The soil consists of clay and lime, on top of soft chalk with black silex (onyx). This combination is very rare in the Champagne and contributes to the unique taste profile.
grape varieties	Chardonnay, from 40-year-old vines
type	extra brut
production	Since 2004, maturation for 36 months *sur lattes* after one year of storage in barrels.

LES MAILLONS, BLANC DE NOIRS
(SÉZANNAIS)

terroir	Single vineyard. The plot is in the Sézanne region and faces east.
soil	The soil is deeper here, and the clay is rich in iron. The layer underneath is chalky. These elements bring out the full taste of the Pinot Noir.
grape varieties	Pinot Noir, from 45-year-old vines
type	extra brut
production	Since 2006, the wine is vinified in oaken barrels and is stored for 11 months. After that it is kept *sur lattes* for 36 months.

LES ENFERS, BLANC DE BLANCS
(COTEAU DU MORIN)

terroir	Single vineyard. The plot is planted on the slopes of Congy next to Les Roises and faces east.
soil	The soil has a top layer of red clay with Campanian chalk underneath.
grape varieties	Chardonnay, from 40-year-old vines
type	extra brut
production	The wine is vinified in oaken barrels and the malolactic fermentation is partial. It is neither clarified nor filtered, and is left to rest for 72 months *sur lattes*.

LES ROISES, BLANC DE BLANCS
(COTEAU DU MORIN)

terroir	Single vineyard. The plot is planted on the slopes of Congy and faces south.
grape varieties	100% Chardonnay, from 65-year-old vines
type	extra brut
production	The wine is vinified in oak and stored for 18 months. Maturation *sur lattes* of 48 months. Limited edition of 3,600 bottles a year.

LES MAILLONS, ROSÉ DE SAIGNÉE
(SÉZANNAIS)

dosage	2.4 g/litre
type	extra brut

CHAMPAGNE CÉDRIC BOUCHARD

**Cédric Bouchard,
a rising star in Champagne**

Cédric Bouchard is a reserved man. If you contact him, do not be surprised if he does not respond, at least not immediately. The reason for this is simple: he has only a limited supply of wine. That is why he does not like tastings, and so for the past two years he has been able to hold them only twice. 'I do not want to disappoint people by telling them a story if I have no wine for them to taste', he says.

Finally, he was charmed by the reason for our visit, namely to write a book about the best champagnes. If he did not want to be included in this book, then the book was not worth writing. This remark broke the ice.

Cédric Bouchard started as a *caviste* in Paris, but quickly realized that he would rather make wine himself than sell it. He received his training in Beaune, in Burgundy. Bouchard is one of the rising stars of the champagne world, a man who always needs challenges.

His initial project was the Inflorescence cuvée. These plots were owned by his father and he has since purchased them. The Inflorescence cuvée no longer exists, since replaced by 'Roses de Jeanne, Côte de Val Vilaine' and 'Roses de Jeanne, Côte des Béchalins'. The name "Roses de Jeanne" refers to the roses you find in the vineyard and to Cédric's grandmother Jeanne, a lady of Polish origin. He consciously did not choose the name Bouchard, as there are many Bouchards around, so with the name of 'Roses de Jeanne' he has clearly distanced himself from them.

Récoltant manipulant
15,000 bottles

Champagne Cédric Bouchard
13, rue des Viviers
F–10110 CELLES-SUR-OURCE
+ 33 3 25 29 69 78
www.champagne-rosesdejeanne.fr

Cédric works on the estate with his cousin Guillaume, who has worked at the Mortet estate in Burgundy, and with his wife, Émilie. Everything is done manually, down to the labelling, rolling the bottles in silk paper and nailing the boxes. In 2000, Cédric had his own label made. The mass of information on it makes it difficult to read.

Cédric opts for partial vineyards with only one grape variety. He chooses Pinot Noir, Pinot Meunier and Chardonnay. He is always looking for individual champagnes, with their own identity. This means monocépages, that is: one plot, one grape, one year. He chooses wines where the vintage or terroir is in the forefront, rather than of assembly wine, of which you never know exactly what's in it. Each wine is made from the first pressing, with spontaneous fermentation and no added sugar. The absence of added sugar better expresses the unique character of each terroir. For Cédric, only the highest quality counts.

After harvest, three pressings are done, of which only the first is used. The must is immediately placed in vats and the champagne is stored in stainless steel *cuves*. Why stainless steel? Because he does not like *la bulle* (bubbles) and wood.

He works biologically and selects the grapes meticulously. He lets nature do her job and never intervenes, or only in exceptional circumstances. It even happens that there is no *soustirage*, meaning that the wine remains *sur lies* (the *lies* or 'lees' is the yeast sediment) until bottling. When the *lie* becomes too thick, it is removed.

Cédric therefore devotes a lot of work to the cellar and opts for a long, slow, cold fermentation. As a result, the champagne has fewer bubbles and is somewhat winey, with a beautiful depth. A minimum of sulphite is added in order to respect and safeguard the work. It may sound selfish, but Cédric only makes champagne that he likes.

→
The rare Pinot Blanc from Cédric Bouchard's small vinotheque

↓
Tasting with Cédric Bouchard in his old cellar at Landreville

P.D
2005

Roses de Jeanne
Champagne

These meticulous working methods mean that the house has a dramatically low return, the lowest in Champagne. Bouchard produces four times less than a regular champagne producer, just 15,000 bottles from 3.45 hectares. The average age of the old vines is 35 years.

In 2008, Gault Millau designated him the most sublime champagne producer, with the finest wines.

We visit his cellar in Landreville, in a beautiful house where the family lives temporarily. Lack of space in Celles-sur-Ource has forced them to move to Landreville. Later they will move back to Celles-sur-Ource. The house in Landreville dates back to the 1800s, originally belonging to Arsène Olivier, a Parisian lawyer, politician, and designer of metro stations. The house was a weekend house and it was decorated with modern gadgets for that time. You could call the servants in the cellar by pressing a button in the salon with your foot, there was steam heating and showers that worked by gravity. Cédric has plans to turn the property into a guesthouse for colleagues from the industry, suppliers, journalists and so on.

The cellar at the house is super. There are no smells. At the tasting, a bat even joins us. Their cellars' great age makes them the ideal place to store the wine. But Cédric has little stock, and if anyone could deliver him a Roses de Jeanne Creux d'Enfer, he'd be very pleased.

Conclusion

Cédric Bouchard is a fantastic champagne maker. He tells us that his champagne may be decanted and he himself opts for a simple wine glass rather than a champagne glass.

Cédric confides in us that he is currently working on a project in the Chablis, Côtes de Nuits, in the village of Molène with mainly Pinot Noir. It is a piece of land from the Cistercians.

We really recommend you to keep this man, his champagne and projects in your sights.

Champagne Cédric Bouchard

CUVÉES AND MILLÉSIMÉS

Roses de Jeanne, Côte de Val Vilaine, Blanc de Noirs

Successor to the Infloresence cuvée

terroir	1.5 hectare plot in Val Vilaine
grape varieties	100% Pinot Noir
dosage	0 g/litre
production	3,600 to 6,000 bottles a year

Roses de Jeanne, Côte des Béchalins, Blanc de Noirs

Successor to the Infloresence cuvée

terroir	1.5 hectare plot on Côte des Béchalins
grape varieties	100% Pinot Noir
production	This champagne lies *sur lies* for three years and is always bottled as a vintage cuvée. Around 1,800 bottles a year.

Roses de Jeanne, Les Ursules, Blanc de Noirs

terroir	0.9 hectare plot
grape varieties	100% Pinot Noir
production	This champagne was produced for the first time in 2014. Around 3,000 to 3,600 bottles a year.

Roses de Jeanne, La Haute Lemblée, Blanc de Blancs

terroir	The grapes come from five 0.5 hectare plots.
grape varieties	100% Chardonnay
production	This champagne is limited.

Roses de Jeanne, La Bolorée, Blanc de Blancs

terroir	This is a very old and rare Pinot Blanc from a 21.7 are plot. Initially, Cédric was not interested in this plot. Three identical lots were sold and straws were drawn. Cédric pulled the shortest straw and came into possession of this little plot.
soil	The soil contains a vein of limestone, which gives the champagne its minerality.
grape varieties	100% Pinot Blanc
results	We have a preference for this champagne.

Roses de Jeanne, Le Creux d'Enfer, Rosé de Saignée

terroir	a rosé champagne made of 100% Pinot Noir from a 7 are plot
grape varieties	100% Pinot Noir
production	The Pinot Noir grape is crushed and there is no skin maceration. No red wine is added. Cédric tells us that this is a very difficult process, which also makes it a rare product.

CHAMPAGNE

CHAMPAGNE FLEURY COURTERON

**Jean-Sébastien Fleury,
a biodynamic wine-growing
pioneer since 1989**

↑
Jean-Sebastien
Fleury, a pioneer
of biodynamic
growing in
Champagne

We drive to the southernmost region of Champagne, the Aube. This is the region of the Côte des Bar, between Bar-sur-Seine, Bar-sur-Aube and Les Riceys, in the Troyes district. We are closer here to Chablis than to Reims, just eight kilometres from the border with Burgundy. In the past, Burgundy began closer to Bar-sur-Seine. With the French Revolution, the borders of Champagne were redrawn further to the south.

In Courteron, a small village with a few side streets and 120 inhabitants, we go looking for the Fleury champagne house. I first tasted this champagne at the Gabbro restaurant in Lille and at Table d'Amis in Kortrijk. I was immediately sold and soon I had made an appointment with the Fleury family.

On the wall of the cellar stands *'Biodynamie depuis 1989'*. The intrusive text makes me somewhat sceptical, but we remain curious.

We are received with a broad smile by Jean-Sébastien Fleury, a sympathetic man who clearly enjoys life. He is the son of the house and also the leading figure in the estate. Born in 1976, he is one of the young generation of winegrowers.

Champagne house Fleury originated in 1895, four generations ago. Great-grandfather was a *pépiniériste* and grape grower. *Pépiniériste* means 'tree grower', but also a breeder of grape vines. Great-grandfather and grandfather struggled to have the Aube included in the champagne region. Fleury is located in the Côte des Bar, and geologically most of this area dates back to the Kimmeridgian era. This era is named after the village of Kimmeridge in England.

Récoltant manipulant
200,000 bottles

Champagne Fleury Courteron
43, Grande Rue
F–10250 COURTERON
+33 03 25 38 20 28
www.champagne-fleury.fr

A Kimmeridge soil, consisting of a compression of small fossilized *exogyra virgula* oysters, formed here about 157-150 million years ago. You can taste this when drinking the champagne, which has an attractive minerality. At Fleury we are on Kimmeridge clay of at least 45 centimetres, at other times of at least 110 centimetres. There are also plots where the soil dates from the Portland period. This soil type is slightly younger and consequently produces less complex wine.

Jean-Sebastian tells us that he works closely with his father Jean-Pierre, and his brother Benoît. His sister Morgane takes care of the commercial side. In this way the estate is being piloted towards the following generation.

Jean-Sebastian's father is an astronomer. For a long time he wanted to do something with the stars and his vineyard. In 1989, this champagne house was the first to work biodynamically on 3 hectares. In 1992, they completely switched to biodynamic wine-growing and in 1994 were certified. Jean-Sébastien, formerly a computer programmer, started in 2009 with vinification in the vineyard.

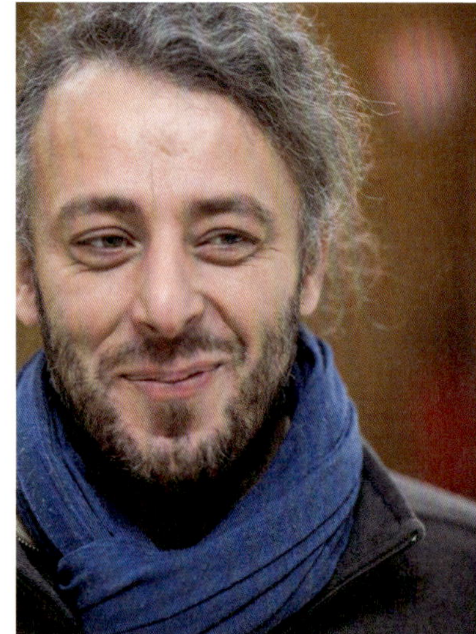

54
CPN Valprune Royat
le 17/09 = 994

During our tour, we arrive in the big shed where a *Coquard* horizontal press from 1990 immediately strikes us. The *Coquard* is one of the most classical presses, in which the juice comes into immediate contact with oxygen. This can be dangerous for oxidation, but oxygen can also stimulate the must. A traditional process that is to be expected here, given this house's great love for the vineyard, nature and ecology. The winery is on a slope, allowing it to work with gravity. This is a feature prized by many winegrowers. In this way, the harvest arrives on a higher level where the grapes are pressed and the juice flows down to a lower floor. This obviates the need to pump. And however soft a pump is, it wears the wine. It is also clear that fifty percent of the quality of champagne is determined by the pressing.

Fleury owns 15 hectares and purchases for 7 hectares from two biodynamic winegrowers.

Today, Fleury produces between 180,000 and 220,000 bottles, half of it for export. The house exports to Hong Kong, Singapore, Japan, the USA, Canada, Brazil, Scandinavia and other European countries. Most foreigners know the Fleury house through the 'Cave Fleury' run by sister Morgane in Paris.

The house employs fifteen people, seven of whom work continuously in the vineyard and in the cellars. All millésimés are corked prior to *dégorgement*. Ten percent is vinified in the barrel, sixty-five barrels in all. All wines undergo malolactic fermentation. Ripening in the bottle can take up to ten years.

Today, Fleury has on average five years' champagnes in stock. The entry champagne is stored for three years. Since 2007, they have had new 60-hectolitre *foudres*, made by house Vicard in Cognac, a must for reserve wine. Reserve wines are stored according to the solera system, especially known for sherry.

Conclusion   The département of Aube may be far from Reims, the current centre of Champagne, but the quality of Champagne Fleury is top.

Wine ageing
'sur lattes'

CUVÉES AND MILLÉSIMÉS

Blanc de Noirs

grape varieties	100% Pinot Noir
assembly	30% reserve wine
dosage	7.5 g/litre
type	brut

Fleur de l'Europe

grape varieties	85% Pinot Noir, 15% Chardonnay
type	brut

Rosé de Saignée

grape varieties	100% Pinot Noir
type	brut

Cépages blancs 2005

grape varieties	100% Chardonnay
type	extra brut

Trilogie 1995

grape varieties	80% Pinot Noir, 20% Chardonnay
type	this millésime exists in three different dosages: extra brut, brut and doux
results	authentic wine; freshness, length; honey and gingerbread

Robert Fleury 2005

grape varieties	35% Pinot Noir, 12% Pinot Meunier, 25% Chardonnay, 28% Pinot Noir
dosage	2.9 g/litre
type	extra brut

Boléro 2005

grape varieties	100% Pinot Noir
dosage	3.8 g/litre
type	extra brut

Notes Blanches, Blanc de Blancs

grape varieties	100% Pinot Noir
type	brut nature

Sonate n° 9, Blanc de Noirs

grape varieties	100% Pinot Noir
type	extra brut nature
results	rich

Complantée
Les Bacous

CHAMPAGNE ROGER BARNIER

Frédéric Berthelot,
quality without château manners

We are half an hour from the Côte des Blancs. Frédéric Berthelot, fifth generation of the Roger Barnier house founded in 1932, receives us. The house owns various plots in the region of Villevenard. All of them are on slopes. In total, the house owns 8.35 hectares, spread over different villages. Some plots are already one hundred years old, but the vines have an average age of forty years. The first Barnier generation was *récoltant manipulant* with the intention already of making champagne itself. Although the house has absolutely no château manners, it makes outstanding champagnes. They work here using reserve wines with a somewhat craft approach.

Récoltant manipulant

50,000 bottles

Champagne Roger Barnier

30, rue Vigne L'Abesse

F–51270 VILLEVENARD

+ 33 3 26 52 82 77

www.champagne-roger-barnier.fr

During my visit, Frédéric invites me for a picnic on one of the steep slopes in Villevenard. We taste a hugely elegant 100% Pinot Meunier. This champagne is no easy product, but still very accessible to the layman and a pleasant surprise for the expert. The champagnes are attractive while remaining firm and are also made traditionally in the old French style.

Conclusion   With an annual output of 50,000 bottles, this is a small champagne house.

It does not belong to the Côte des Blancs and the Coteaux du Sézannais. The result is a Chardonnay champagne that is more winey than the Chardonnay champagnes of the Côte des Blancs, but more elegant than those of the Coteaux du Sézannais. I can only conclude that Champagne Roger Barnier is one of my favourite champagnes.

↑
View down
the steeply-
sloping vineyard
in Villevenard

↗
Separate tanks
for individual
plots

→
Wine storage
in the amphora
project

CHAMPAGNE
RB
ROGER BARNIER

← ←
The round
Coquard press
at Barnier

↑
A careful eye
is kept on
both vineyard
and cellar

→
Storage in
wooden barrels
at Barnier

←
Frédéric
Barnier and a
close-up of the
Coquard press

↓
Barnier's
first cellar

↘
Pieter Verheyde
and Frédéric
Barnier in the
sur lattes room

CUVÉES AND MILLÉSIMÉS

Roger Barnier Cuvée Sélection

grape varieties	10% Pinot Noir, 32% Pinot Meunier, 58% Chardonnay

Cuvée Les Nuits Blanches

terroir	The grapes come from three different plots, Le Perrier, Les Foulonnes and Les Greffières.
grape varieties	100% Chardonnay
assembly	millésime
dosage	low dosage
production	This champagne is aged in the barrel and has a low sugar dosage.
results	This champagne, available only in magnums, is dedicated to the festival of Les Nuits Blanches.

Cuvée Exquise, 2006

terroir	The grapes come from different plots: Chardonnay from Le Perrier and Les Greffières, Pinot Meunier from Les bas jardins and Les Clos-prieurs, Pinot Noir from Les Marboutteries
grape varieties	25% Pinot Noir tête de cuvée, 5% Pinot Meunier tête de cuvée, 70% Chardonnay tête de cuvée, The tête de cuvée is the first juice tapped.
type	brut
result	This is a traditional champagne with an average age of 10 years. The house was looking for an excellent champagne and therefore named it 'Exquise'.

Cuvée Blanche

terroir	The Chardonney grapes come from the Le Perrière, La Vigne aux Moines and Les Greffières plots.
Grape varieties	100% Chardonnay
assembly	millésime
production	The champagne is vinified by plot, with half of it stored in barrels.

Cuvée Rosé Le Magnum

type	brut
production	Little of this champagne is produced, there are few bottles. This champagne is lively and is made from the Brut Sélection and 16% red wine based on old vines.

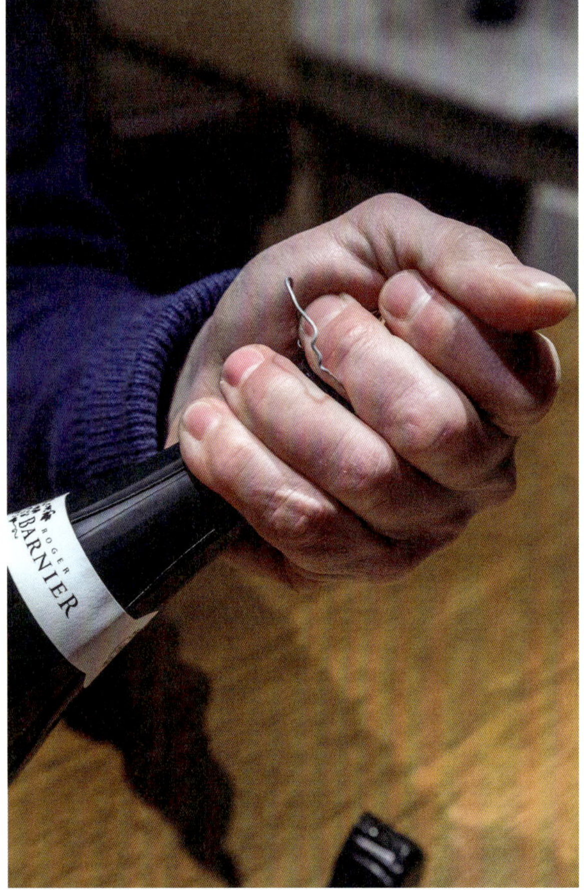

CHAMPAGNE
JACQUES LASSAIGNE
MONTGUEUX

CHAMPAGNE JACQUES LASSAIGNE MONTGUEUX

**Emmanuel Lassaigne:
gastronomy and precision**

It's a long drive to the village of Montgueux, just west of Troyes, the former capital of Champagne and once famous for its clothing industry.

On my way, I notice how many winegrowers here are named Lassaigne, perhaps all related. We have a rendezvous with Emmanuel Lassaigne, the son of the house who has set the domain on a clear course into the future.

We drive into the estate and his mother comes striding towards us. A soft-spoken woman, she invites us through to a room at the back of the house where her son is.

My attention is drawn by a field in front of the house. It is covered with old moss-covered vines: a fairy-tale image, magical and inviting. Even if the signboard looks more like that of a Mercure Hotel, do not be deceived…

Emmanuel, the founder's son, awaits us. He comes across as a closed man with a strict and investigative look, a man who likes to wait to try to find out with some direct remarks with whom he is dealing. The conversation gets moving slowly but surely. He tells me that his great-grandfather came to Montgueux after the First World War because he was in love with the daughter of one of the town's main figures. He was a mere farm labourer… The class difference was great, but their love was even greater. His great-grandparents had thirteen children. This immediately explains the large presence of the Lassaigne clan.

Négociant manipulant

50,000 bottles

Champagne Jacques Lassaigne

7, chemin des Haies

10300 MONTGUEUX

+33 3 25 74 84 83

www.montgueux.com

Montgueux has 215 hectares of vineyards and 80 winemakers, spread across south and southeast facing hills. It is the only wine region in Champagne which is isolated, which has its benefits in terms of viticulture. The immense chalk mountain is an outcrop of the Côte des Blancs, but 15 million years older. Long ago, there was a sea here, hence the brine, iodine and marine influences. The Côte des Bar, on the other hand, has a clay and lime soil, giving a completely different wine style.

The region around Montgueux has always been agricultural, and it is a coincidence that there is still wine growing here. The peasant families provided for their own needs and thus made their own wine. Winegrowing was not as sexy then as it is now, and in order not to pay taxes, the surrounding *communes* decided to relinquish their AOC (*appellation originale contrôlée*) in 1927. Only Montgueux did not. Three notables fought to maintain the AOC.

Montgueux is known as the Montrachet of Champagne, with almost exclusively Chardonnay vines.

In 1964, the Lassaigne founded their wine-growing business, initially only with still wines, no champagne. The sparkling part of the story started only in the 1980s. Most local farmers sell their grapes to large houses in Reims or Épernay.

Emmanuel has worked for ten years outside the wine industry. It intrigues us how he can deliver such a good product. 'Un coup de bol' (luck), he laughs. Passion, curiosity and perseverance are the driving force. Nor was his father trained as a winemaker. 'But we're locals', he says.

The domain covers 3.5 hectares, and produces about 50,000 bottles. There are only three employees. 'Small', I say. 'Enough and not bad', he replies.

Right in front of the house is the plot of Le Cotet. This is also the name of the place where the estate is located, on the edge of the village.

→
Moss-covered
vines of the
'Le Cotet' plot

↓
Emmanuel
Lassaigne,
a one-off but driven
winemaker

The label mentions *'négociant manipulant'* because the house also purchases some grapes from other vineyards. The criteria for these purchased grapes are strict: old vines, *sélection massale*, processed according to their own specifications. In Montgueux everyone knows everyone and the cooperation is good. To the question of whether he would like more land he answers: 'Not really, unless an opportunity crops up. But there is little land available.'

Strikingly, Montgueux never suffers water shortages. Chalk can easily hold 60% water. Even a three-month drought in 2015 did no damage.

In the vineyard, there is natural grass growth, no cultivation, resulting in different root growth. The grass is not mowed, only the fibres are repeatedly broken with a roller. The grass is flattened and the energy passes into the roots, producing biological activity in the soil.

Lassaigne is not bio-certified. 'But we never add compost or artificial fertilizer. For ten years now, we have not used herbicides or insecticides, not even bio-products. Because we do not use manure, there is no overly strong growth. The vines have a hard time of it, but they are disease-resistant. We can of course have mildew, that's climatological, but we've not had any rot since 2001. Nor are we influenced by nearby vineyards.'

Montgueux is high up and catches a lot of wind so that diseases get less chance. '*Chefs de caves* sometimes come and tell me what I should do differently, or what to add, but I don't follow their advice and it's better that way.' Large houses need to produce rapidly and in large quantities. At Lassaigne, this is not the case. 'We have time and we are not looking for big production.'

Wine making is reduced to the strictly necessary. Pressing, light *débourbage*, natural fermentation. Afterwards, the production from each plot goes partly into a barrel and partly into a *cuve*. At Lassaigne, there is no classification to distinguish between cheap, average and top cuvée. All wines are vinified by plot and come from five plots:

› Le Cotet: old vines,
› Grande Côte: planted in 1963,
› La Voie Creuse: planted in 1955,
› Les Paluets: 60 years old,
› Clos Sainte-Sophie: planted between 1968 and 1975.

There are three methods for ripening on yeast:
› Les Vignes de Montgueux: 2 to 2.5 years ripening,
› La Colline inspirée, Le Cotet, Les Papilles Insolites: 3 to 4 years ripening,
› The Millésimés: 6, 7 or 8 years ripening.

Remuage is done with a *gyropalette*, a device in which 504 bottles are constantly moved to a particular pattern.

Dégorgement is done manually, *à la volée*, without a freeze bath. No sulphite or liqueur is added. If you *dégorge* properly, there is no need to add any *liqueur d'expédition* or extra liquid. The *prise de mousse* increases the volume. Less yeast, less *prise de mousse*, so less loss. Unheard of. *Chefs de caves* from the big houses come here to see and say it can't be done. For the past five years, all wines have been *zero dosage*, i.e. no added sugar.

25% of the wines are sold in Paris, mainly through cellar owners. For this reason, after *dégorgement* the wine has a further formation period in the bottle: Les Vignes de Montgueux: 4 months, Le Cotet, La Colline inspirée, Les Papilles Insolites: 6 months to 1 year and the Millésimés: 1 year.

In this way, when the bottle arrives at the *caviste* or sommelier, it is fully formed and quickly ready to drink.

'I have no bad years', says Emmanuel, 'every year is different, no one year is the same. In the large houses, the *chefs de cave* decide at harvest time whether to make a millésimé or not; I make a millésimé every year. 2003 was the year of the heatwave, yet that wine is so beautiful today. 2008 was overall a good year, but 80% of the grapes were damaged by hail and yet we made a millésimé. I realize that what I say cannot be done everywhere, not everywhere are there optimal climatic conditions.'

Emmanuel confesses: 'In the Champagne region it's easy to earn a pile of money. Everyone knows the recipe for this. I've not opted to get rich quick. I've chosen a lifestyle.'

CUVÉES AND MILLÉSIMÉS

Les Vignes de Montgueux, Blanc de Blancs

assembly	An assembly of 7 to 9 plots with wine from two consecutive years.
type	extra brut
results	An aperitif cuvée, with freshness, minerality and citrus fruit. A fresh and pure champagne.

Les Papilles Insolites

terroir	Pinot Noir from the Montgueux chalk soil
soil	chalk
grape varieties	Pinot Noir
type	extra brut
results	natural, winey, fruity wine: wild nose with red fruit as mouth sensation. Les Papilles Insolites no longer exists since 2012

Le Cotet, Blanc de Blancs

terroir	Le Cotet plot. 40-year-old vines anchored in chalk on the eastern slope of the village.
soil	chalk
type	extra brut
results	Mineral, very fresh with lemon as mouth sensation. Ideal with oysters and seafood.

La Colline inspirée, Blanc de Blancs

type	extra brut
results	A champagne with Burgundian allures. Exotic touch and freshness with touches of toasted brioche.

Millésime 2000, Blanc de Blancs

grape varieties	100% Chardonnay
type	brut nature
results	for large gatherings, aperitifs or meal; freshness and length, honey and gingerbread; authentic wine

Millésime 2002, Blanc de Blancs

grape varieties	100% Chardonnay
type	brut nature
results	finesse from bubble to bubble, very rich with butter taste, fruit and balanced, white truffle

Millésime 2003, Blanc de Blancs

assembly	atypical year; wine from old vines from two plots
type	brut nature
results	nose of ripe fruit, honey and candied quince

Millésime 2004, Blanc de Blancs

grape varieties	100% Chardonnay
type	brut nature
results	full and complete, licorice, a terroir for aperitif, fresh and winey.

Millésime 2005, Blanc de Blancs

grape varieties	100% Chardonnay
type	brut nature
results	rich year, full wine; mandarin and melon; extravagance for one year with increased sensation

Rosé de Montgueux

grape varieties	Pinot Noir, Chardonnay
type	extra brut rosé
results	raspberry, vine peach and wild strawberry: a Pinot Noir vinified as red wine for the fruity aromas, on a base of Chardonnay grapes from old vines for freshness, finesse and balance. Rosé de Montgueux no longer exists since 2012

Coteaux Champenois Blanc, Blanc de Blancs

terroir	Montgueux
results	White wine for large tables. In this still wine you taste the terroir of Montgueux and the signature of the Jacques Lassaigne house.

CHAMPAGNE DIEBOLT-VALLOIS

I met Jacques Diebolt for the first time in 1997, when working for Alain Ducasse in the eponymous restaurant in Paris. I had planned a weekend in Champagne and wanted to get off the beaten track and do some discovering. And what a discovery! I joined a small group, including a number of Belgians, and ended up at Diebolt-Vallois. The absolute highlight was a 1953 bottle we degorged by hand, à la *volée*. This means removing the yeast still in the bottle, in the final stage before adding the *liqueur d'expédition*, a technique rarely used today. The cork is drawn out of the bottle with pincers, and the pressure forces out the yeast nestling under it. This is done in a fraction of a second so as to minimize the loss.

Until today, the taste of that champagne has remained with me. What a rich, elegant style! In addition, I discovered two flavours I had never perceived before in champagne, paprika powder and roast pork. What an experience...

Twenty years after I was surprised by the 1953, I got the chance to taste it again with Jacques, 'but it'll be the last time' he warns. We descend into the cellar, search and find the bottle. It looks intact, apart from the metal ring holding the cork in place that has rusted through and hangs by one leg. We open the bottle again à la *volée*, and the yeast cells fly around. What we taste is unbelievable, with a tertiary nose of boletus. Absolute top. The iron had not withstood the tooth of time, but the champagne was even better. Over 60 years old and in top form!

Champagne Diebolt-Vallois

84, rue Neuve

F–51530 Cramant

+33 3 26 57 54 92

www.diebolt-vallois.com

When working at a boutique restaurant at Melrose Place in Los Angeles, I came across the house once again via a wine importer lady friend. Since then, I've never lost sight of Diebolt. From Los Angeles via Kruishoutem to Watou. The champagne from Cramant is as elegant as ever, with a nose of citrus and chalk. Cramant boasts many other tasty champagnes, but Diebolt places the bar slightly higher. The wines are very discreet when young, but with huge storage potential.

The Diebolt-Vallois family estate is located in Cramant, on the Côte des Blancs.

The hilly region around the village derives its name from the limestone soil. In some places, a 200-metre deep layer of lime lies concealed under just 25 centimetres of earth. The belemnite chalk is crumbly and so porous that you can easily write with it. This geological phenomenon provides one of the most attractive terroirs of the Côte des Blancs. Travelling from Épernay, Cramant is one of the first grand cru villages of the Côte des Blancs, just past the premier cru village of Cuis. All vineyards are 100% grand cru.

Jacques Diebolt grew up in Cramant, and married Nadia Vallois, from the neighbouring village of Cuis. Jacques is a fascinating and seductive man who awakens this passion in you as he talks about his style and the village of Cramant. His motto: *"Pour faire du bon, il faut toujours faire mieux"* (To do something good, you must always do something better). He has a catchy enthusiasm – *'Il est touchant'*, they say; but he is also a damn good dealer.

I am honoured to have met this icon. The man has 50 years of wine making to his credit and can tell you everything about climate and production. A living heritage.

The Diebolt family hails from Alsace. During the German occupation at the end of the 19th century, the family moved so as not to live under the yoke of the German occupier. Originally, they were not winemakers: Jacques' ancestors were furniture makers. His grandfather Jules Crepaux became a *vigneron* at Cramant.

The Diebolt family has been making wine since the 19th century, the Vallois family since the 15th century. By inheritance the vineyards were divided up. In 1978, the family invested in a new cellar, reaching 15 metres below the ground, partly into the mother limestone.

As I stand with Jacques on a smallish plot – a *climat* – on the Pimont, he tells me he started working there as a child with his grandfather. 'A hill ridge with an attractive location, here they can bury me', he murmurs...

↗
Old vines in the 'Côte des Blancs' and Jacques Diebolt looking out over one of his vineyards

→
Jacques' beloved Pimont plot in Cramant

→ Bringing in
the harvested
Chardonnay grapes

↘ Perfect hygiene,
a key aspect in the
winery.

→ The harvested grapes
are carried to the press.

↓ Filling the pneumatic
press, view from above

In the family company, daughter Isabelle (°1962) and son Arnaud (°1966) take care of the day-to-day work in the cellars and the vineyards. Only at harvest time do they bring in seasonal workers.

The Diebolt-Vallois house produces about 1,115 hectolitres annually, which corresponds to 156,000 bottles. They have a solid commercial network, with small volumes dispatched across the world. Walking through the warehouse, I see shipments ready for Sweden, one of their best markets, Norway, Greenland, Japan and South Korea.

The Diebolt-Vallois estate covers 14 hectares. Most of the vineyards are located on the Côte des Blancs, mainly on grand cru and premier cru plots in Cuis and Cramant. Others are on the Coteaux d'Épernay, in the hamlets of Les Toulettes and Les Hautes Justices.

Recent vines – Pinot Noir and Pinot Meunier – have been added on the Montagne de Reims and the Côte des Bar plots. Jacques recounts a recent purchase: the current per hectare price of Cramant grand cru land is (2017) 1.8 million euros, that of premier cru in Cuis 1.5 million.

Because the vineyards of Cramant are very close to those of Avize, we do not talk about the specific characteristics of the *commune*, but rather about the characteristics of the vineyard and its exposure. The vineyards are oriented south-east. There is just a small surface layer of earth, and here and there fragmented chalk betrays its presence.

Vignes à Cuis (premier cru)
Cuis lies next to Cramant. Here the plots face in different directions: northwest and south, again on chalk. This ensures minerality and lightness. The grapes of the Coteaux d'Epernay give equilibrium, roundness and volume.

The grapes are picked by hand. The family keeps the harvests from each plot separate to process them separately into champagne.

For the pressing stage, they use a traditional vertical and a modern pneumatic press. Thus they keep the cuvées (juice of the first pressing) for all blancs de blancs. The alcoholic fermentation proceeds according to the needs of the cuvée: either in temperature controlled vats or in barrels. All cuvées undergo malolactic fermentation, except Fleur de Passion.

The reserves are stored in *foudres* or in large 86 hectolitre vats for slow, regular ripening. These impart a round, warm touch to the champagne of the Diebolt-Vallois house.

After bottling, the champagnes complete their second fermentation and their *prise de mousse* in the estate's cellars, where they remain for a number years before *dégorgement*. The dosage is on average between six to eight grams per litre.

→
The master's eye shows us the dead yeast in the neck.

↓
Pieter Verheyde and Jacques Diebolt tasting one of the last bottles of the extremely rare "1953".

↙
The dead yeast is clearly visible against the neck of the bottle after gradual rotation (*remuage*).

CUVÉES AND MILLÉSIMÉS

Fleur de Passion, Blanc de Blancs

classification	grand cru
terroir	The grapes come from seven to eight plots on the slopes of Cramant, more specifically from the hamlet of Les Buzons. The yields are low, the quality all the higher. The general orientation of the plots is east and east-south-east.
grape varieties	100% Chardonnay from on average 65-year-old vines
assembly	millésime
dosage	6 to 8 g/litre
type	brut
production	The 1995 millésime is the first year of Fleur de Passion. The champagne is stored in oak barrels, creating a good interaction with oxygen. This is of course not a new method. The barrels themselves are never new. The alcoholic fermentation takes place in *barriques* that have already had several wines. No malolactic fermentation, no filtering, no collage. Everything that can disturb the wine is avoided to optimize the terroir experience. Storage is in Burgundy *barriques*.
results	Fleur de Passion is the pearl of the Diebolt-Vallois house. The family produces six to seven thousand bottles of it a year. Having the quality fruit in house, they could increase production, but they also use the high quality grapes for other cuvées. Fleur de Passion is a violent, elegant lady with fresh acids, because she does not undergo malolactic fermentation, collage or filtration. Fleur de Passion flowers only in the best wine years. In 2001, 2003 and 2009 none was made.
serving	Serve the champagne in summer at 9°C, in winter at 10-11°C. Pour the champagne into a carafe 15 minutes in advance for a better expression.

Prestige, Blanc de Blancs

classification	grand cru
terroir	Cramant, Chouilly and Le Mesnil-sur-Oger, three large cru villages; east-south-east facing plots
soil	thin layer of earth on a chalk base
grape varieties	100% Chardonnay
assembly	assembly of three years kept in newish oak *foudres*.
dosage	6 to 8 g/litre
production	Fermentation takes place in thermo-regulated vats.
results	round, rich, complex.
serving	Serve the champagne in summer at 9°C, in winter at 10-11°C.

Millésimé, Blanc de Blancs

classification	premier cru
terroir	Cuis, Chouilly, Epernay and young vines from Cramant.
soil	thin layer of topsoil on a chalk base
grape varieties	100% Chardonnay
assembly	millésime
type	brut
dosage	6 to 8 g/litre
production	The Blanc de Blancs Millésimé is produced only if the grape quality is good enough. Fermentation takes place in thermo-regulated vats.
results	round, rich, complex.
serving	Serve the champagne in summer at 9°C, in winter at 10-11°C.

Blanc de Blancs

classification	premier cru
terroir	Cuis, Chouilly, Epernay and young vines from Cramant.
grape varieties	100% Chardonnay
assembly	assembly of two years
dosage	6 to 8 g/litre
type	brut
production	Fermentation in thermo-regulated vats
results	vibrant and elegant, suitable for an aperitif or starting the meal
serving	Serve the champagne in summer at 9°C, in winter at 10-11°C.

Rosé

classification	grand cru
terroir	Largely from Les Toulettes in Épernay.
grape varieties	63% Pinot Noir, 10% Pinot Meunier, 27% Chardonnay
dosage	7 g/litre
type	brut rosé
production	Fermentation in thermo-regulated vats; rosé assembly, with the addition of Bouzy Rouge (grand cru)
results	Elegant and fruity with aromas of raspberry, wild strawberry and redcurrants. A joyful champagne, ideal as an aperitif or in summertime in the garden.
serving	Serve the champagne in summer at 9°C, in winter at 10-11°C.

Tradition

classification	grand cru
terroir	originating from different terroirs on the domain
grape varieties	30 to 40% Pinot Noir, 20 to 30% Pinot Meunier, 40% Chardonnay
assembly	millésime
dosage	6 to 8 g/litre
type	brut
production	Fermentation in thermo-regulated vats
results	Balanced champagne, ideal as an aperitif or at the start of a meal
serving	Serve the champagne in summer at 9°C, in winter at 10-11°C.

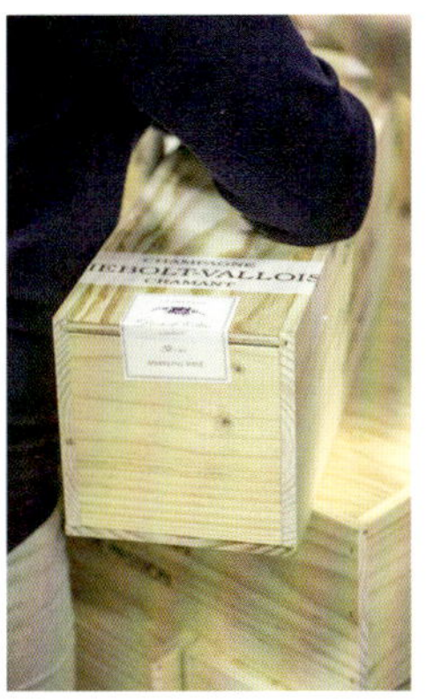

CHAMPAGNE DAVID LÉCLAPART

Only in 2010 did I get to know Léclapart, which is pretty late, given that David is already the fourth generation of this champagne house. In Trépail, near Ambonnay,

we come across this colourful house on a corner of the street. A charming but certainly not flamboyant building. Here they make very pure, elegant wine.

The Léclapart house is a one-man shop, a *maison* in the true sense of the word, because it is no more than that. The logo shows the wheel of life, the balance between water, earth, wind and fire. David Léclapart is a man of sober approach and extreme precision. His wines bear witness to a consistent attitude. A man in his late forties, with grey curls and a friendly expression receives us. He seems to me a very sensitive person. In a soft voice he tells me his story.

'I'd finished my general studies, nothing to do with agriculture or oenology. I had a diploma in my pocket, but was unemployed and with not a cent in my pocket. It was a busy period in the parental vineyard and my parents could use some more pairs of hands. So in 1989, I returned home to my parents' winery.' They cultivated the vineyards in traditional style, just as David would later.

He started helping in the vineyard, and though he had never done this kind of work before, he liked it a lot. 'A world opened up for me. But I realized I needed some training and started working at two big houses, Lanson and Pommery, and then at Leclerc-Briant at Épernay. I also took courses at the agricultural school in Beaujeu.'

Champagne David Léclapart

10, rue de la Mairie

F–51380 TRÉPAIL

+33 3 26 57 07 01

David came into contact with biodynamic viticulture and became a big fan of Max Léglise and Rudolf Steiner. In 1996, he lost his father and took over the estate, on the condition that he could work fully biodynamically. Since 2000, his vineyard has been bio-certified and today he works fully biodynamically.

The premier cru village of Trépail is located on the Côte des Noirs. This wine area is planted mainly with Pinot Noir and Pinot Meunier. At Léclapart, however, the Chardonnay grape dominates, as elsewhere in the village. The 22 plots are spread over three hectares. A hectare can produce in principle 3000 bottles, but he produces 15,000. This is due to the *métayage* system (from *moitié*, half). This means that he uses

plots belonging to another owner and is contractually required to pay half of the grapes to him. The other owner is Marguet, a wine producer in Ambonnay.

Owing to lack of space, he makes no millésimés. His champagnes are stored for just fifteen months *sur lies*, not long enough to carry the millésimé label. In this way, the character of the different plots is expressed. On the back label, you can read, however, the year in which the grapes were picked.

David Léclapart is driven in his winemaking by pure energy, pleasure and attention to ecology. He believes in the creative power of biodynamic farming, a combination of water, earth, wind and fire. In the wine cellar, he minimizes his own intervention and he tries to maximize the expression of the characteristics of the particular year.

In this northernmost region of France it is difficult to work biodynamically, says David, making the work in the vineyard itself even more important than elsewhere. 'We have little sunshine, less warmth, and a high risk of mildew. For all these reasons we have to work very precisely.' However, he is convinced that the work in the vineyard decisively impacts the quality in the bottle: 'Everything gained in the vineyard we retain. We take nothing away and do not adjust. We use little sulphur and do not clarify or filter the wine. There is no cold stabilization and we do not promote malolactic fermentation, but we let the wine undergo spontaneous fermentation.

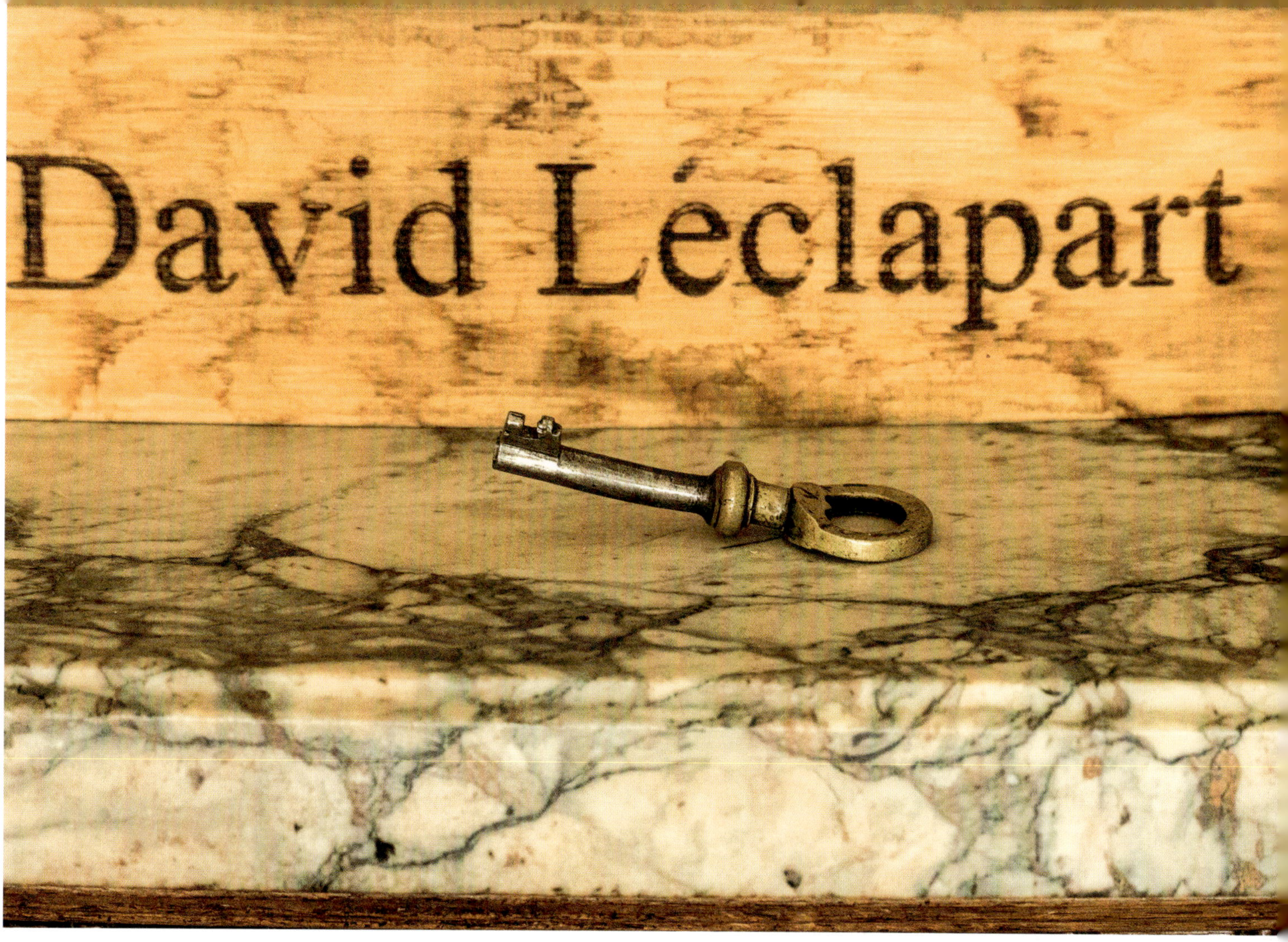
David Léclapart

Champagne
David Léclapart
L'Amateur
Champagne
David Léclapart
L'Artiste
Champagne
David Léclapart
L'Apôtre
Champagne
David Léclapart
L'Alchimiste
Champagne
David Léclapart
TRÉPAIL ROUGE
David Léclapart

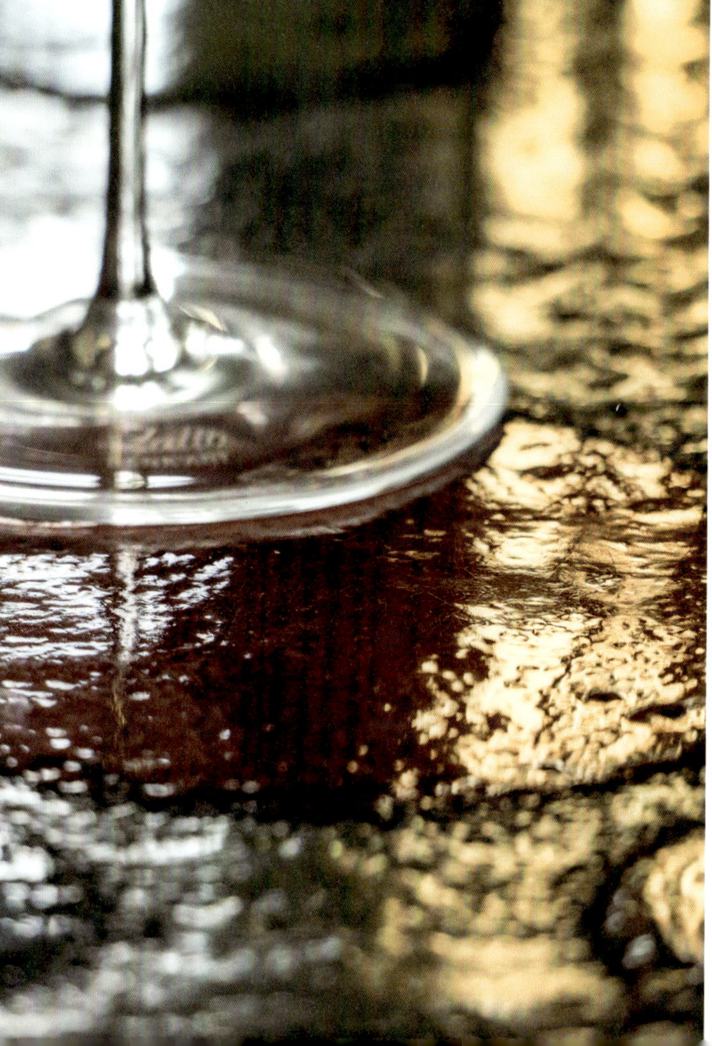

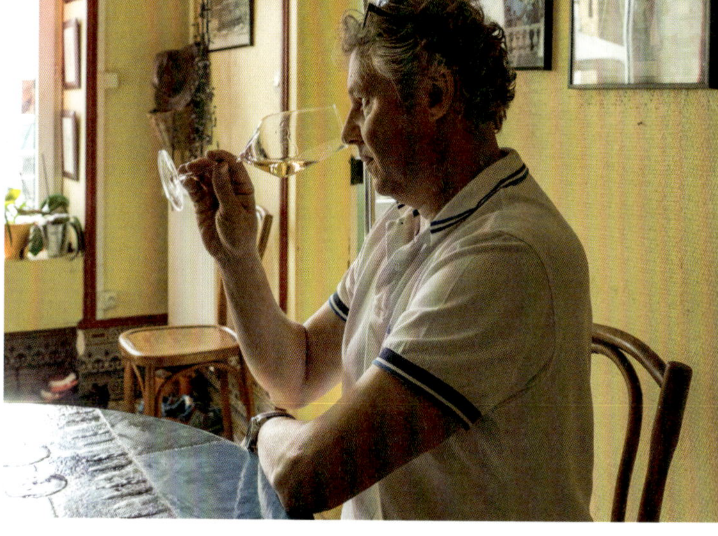

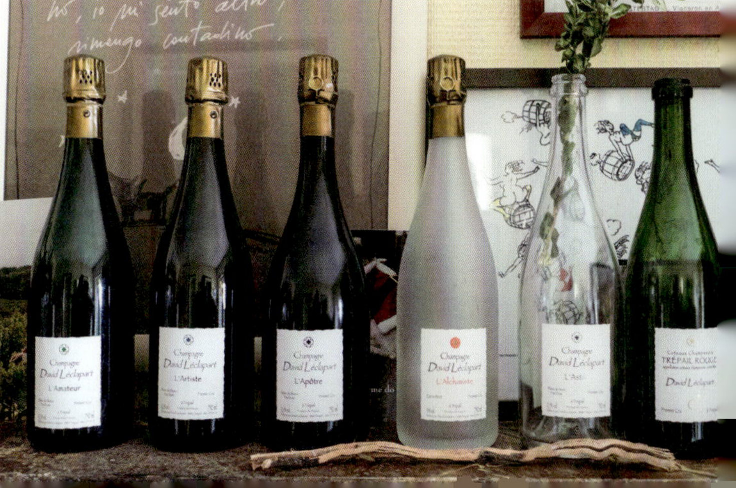

CUVÉES AND MILLÉSIMÉS

David Léclapart makes several cuvées including
three Blanc de Blancs and one Blanc de Noirs.

L'Amateur, Blanc de Blancs

classification | premier cru
terroir | six different lots in Trépail
grape varieties | 100% Chardonnay
type | pas dosé
production | vinified in enamelled steel tanks.

L'Artiste, Blanc de Blancs

classification | premier cru
terroir | selected plots
grape varieties | 100% Chardonnay
type | pas dosé
production | The wine is partially vinified in 228 litre
burgundy barrels, partly in enamelled steel tanks.

L'Apôtre, Blanc de Blancs

classification | premier cru
terroir | the plot La Pierre Saint-Martin, planted
by David's grandfather in 1946
grape varieties | 100% Chardonnay
type | pas dosé
production | The wine is fully vinified in 228 litre neutral
Burgundy vats.

L'Astre, Blanc de Noirs

classification | premier cru
terroir | Originating from four different plots,
one of them dating from the 1950s.
grape varieties | 100% Pinot Noir
type | pas dosé
production | fully vinified in used barrels
results | This cuvée replaces l'Alchimiste, a rosé.
David had trouble keeping the rosé constant
and made a Blanc de Noirs. The intention was to
make a one-off cuvée, like a star appearing once –
hence the name *astre* (star).
This is David's very first Blanc de Noirs.
It has a small rosé touch from the four hour
skin maceration.

L'Alchimiste rosé

classification | premier cru
terroir | plots in Le Champ Janvrai planted in 1957,
and La Fleuranne planted in 1968,
on the southern slopes of Trépail.
grape varieties | 100% Pinot Noir
type | pas dosé
production | The Pinot Noir grapes are stripped,
macerated for 24 to 72 hours in large wooden
barrels and crushed by foot for 4 hours a day.

CHAMPAGNE MINIÈRE F & R

A few miles north of Reims, in the region of the Massif de Saint Thierry, we are received by the brothers Frédéric and Rodolphe Minière, who head up this young champagne house. Their motto: 'Nature as a foundation and beauty as a horizon with the intention of excelling'.

In Hermonville people have been in grape growing since the 12th century. Frédéric and Rodolphe are the fourth generation working on the domaine that is founded in 1919 by their great-grandfather Alfred Darlu-Minière. He owned a press and sold his wines to the *négociants* of Reims. Frédéric and Rodolphe still speak of their great-grandfather with the greatest respect. Over the years, it was their grandparents Henri and Madeleine and afterwards their parents Gérard and Josette who expanded the company. Rodolphe and Frédéric, the fourth generation in the business, both studied oenology in Avize. Frédéric has discovered his passion for the profession at Anselme Selosse with the intention of later making champagne himself.

This the brothers started in 2005 via the co-operative. At the same time, they stopped selling their grapes to *négociants*. Two years later, in 2007, they launched their own label, Champagne Minière F & R.

The two are the first generation to make champagne. They have beautiful, old vines. The company is in full expansion and you feel on the estate that this champagne house will continue to evolve. Frédéric and Rodolphe want to make the most of this particular domain. They have five cuvées from different plots. In the vineyard they work traditionally, with respect for ecology and biological additions. Biodiversity is very important to them. Sustainable viticulture is their motto.

The brothers use wooden barrels of different contents, different origins and different ages.

Champagne Minière F & R

8 bis, rue Saint Martin

F–51220 HERMONVILLE

+ 33 3 26 50 68 43

www.champagne-miniere.fr

At the end of the first pressing, the must is immediately placed into *barriques* for the alcoholic fermentation. The wine is kept for six to eight months *sur lies*. Depending on the year, there is more or less *bâtonnage*. The brothers believe in wine evolving slowly, as this gives greater expression and thus more pleasure to the consumer.

Their goal is to produce about 45,000 bottles a year and to let them age attractively.

The oldest vineyards are in Hermonville and were planted in the 1950s, mainly with Chardonnay and Pinot Meunier. In all, they own 8 hectares of vineyards, of which two are planted with Chardonnay, one with Pinot Noir and the rest with Pinot Meunier. The different plots contain old vines: Les Fauvagnes is planted with Pinot Meunier from 1968 and 1969, and Pinot Meunier with original rootstock from 1962. Les Rosières is planted with Pinot Meunier and Pinot Noir with original rootstock from 1974 and Chardonnay from 1973. Les Grands Blancs: Chardonnay from 1964 and Chardonnay with original rootstock from 1965. Les Fosselles: Pinot Noir from 1975 and Chardonnay from 2003. Les Moineaux: Pinot Meunier from 1963, 1969 and 1971, Pinot Noir from 1981 and Chardonnay from 1963. Les Voirmissa: Pinot Meunier from 1947 and 1967, Pinot Noir from 1968 and Chardonnay from 1972. La Couturelle: Pinot Meunier from 1986, 1987, 1988, 1989, 1990, 1992, 1993 and Pinot Noir from 2002.

Currently 30 percent of their grapes they process themselves, and sell the remaining 70 percent. The vineyards are largely protected by the wind, which is good for combating mould.

During our walk through the vineyards, we notice something strange. There is nothing planted between two plots, which are split apart by a small road. The small passage appears to date from the First World War. Below, behind the cellar, a British Commonwealth graveyard bears silent witness to this Great War.

Conclusion   This is a very young champagne house, with little material to fall back on. The two brothers have already made substantial investments. They intend to keep their wine stored for a long time, for 6 to 10 years. It is a house with a fresh challenge, a surprise in the champagne world. Starting a new house today is a real feat.

During our visit, we asked Frédéric for his preference, but he was unable to answer, as he had not yet tasted everything. They only started marketing their champagne at the end of 2014.

We have enormous respect for the two brothers and their excellent champagnes.

08/09
27/05/16

DYNAMIE DEPU

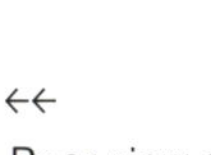

←← Rear view of the Minière house and the adjacent vineyard

↑ Main entrance in the Rue St. Martin in Hermonville

→ *Tâcherons* or seasonal labourers at work in the vineyard

↖ Pieter Verheyde, Rodolphe Minière and dog in the vineyard at Hermonville

↓ Grassing alongside the vineyard to prevent erosion

↘ Storage room to which the harvested grapes are brought immediately

CHAMPAGNE
MINIÈRE F&R

CUVÉES AND MILLÉSIMÉS

Blanc Absolu, Blanc de Blancs

terroir	Grapes from the hamlet of Les Moineaux
grape varieties	100% Chardonnay
assembly	15% reserve wine
dosage	6 g/litre
type	brut
production	Vinification takes place in wooden barrels. No malolactic fermentation. Six years' storage *sur lies*. *Dégorgement* six months before sale.
results	Mineral, complex and toasted nose

Brut Zéro

terroir	The Pinot Noir grapes come from Les Fosselles, the Pinot Meunier grapes come from Les Couturelles, the Chardonnay grapes from Les Fontenelles.
grape varieties	28% Pinot Noir, 45% Pinot Meunier, 27% Chardonnay, 19% reserve wine
assembly	15% reserve wine
dosage	0 g/litre
type	brut nature
production	This champagne is vinified in the barrel without malolactic fermentation. The vinification takes place 30% in new barrels and 70% in four-year-old barrels. Seven years' storage *sur lies*. *Dégorgement* six months before sale.
results	Toasted nose

Symbiose, cuvée millésimée

terroir	The Pinot Noir comes from the hamlet of Les Voirmissa, the Chardonnay from Les Moineaux.
grape varieties	50% Pinot Noir, 50% Chardonnay
assembly	millésime
dosage	2,5 g/litre
type	extra brut
production	Vinification in barrels aged seven years and older. No malolactic fermentation. Stored ten years *sur lies*. *Dégorgement* six months before sale.
results	perfect marriage of Pinot Noir and Chardonnay

Influence Rosé

grape varieties	35% Pinot Noir, 40% Pinot Meunier, 25% Chardonnay, 20% reserve wine
assembly	15% reserve wine.
dosage	8 g/litre
type	brut
production	7% of red wine is added to the white. The wine is 30% vinified in barrels less than four years old and 70% in barrels at least five years old. No malolactic fermentation. Four years' storage *sur lies*. *Dégorgement* six months before sale.

Influence, cuvée brut

terroir	The Pinot Noir comes from Les Fosselles, the Pinot Meunier from Les Couturelles and the Chardonnay from Les Fontenelles.
grape varieties	30% Pinot Noir, 40% Pinot Meunier, 15% Chardonnay, 15% reserve wine
assembly	15% reserve wine
type	brut
results	This is the Minière brothers' flagship. You notice the attractive influence of ageing in wood barrels.

CHAMPAGNE
Francis Boulard

CHAMPAGNE FRANCIS BOULARD & FILLE

Francis Boulard and 'le sens du naturel'

We remain in the Saint-Thierry region, and stop at the house Francis Boulard et Fille. We ring the bell, the door opens and a man, as wide as he is tall, looks at us with suspicious eyes. After introducing ourselves, and answering a series of questions, we

are welcomed. Francis Boulard explains why he was so unaccommodating: every day people come to make contact and ask for (free) tastings. He suspected that this was also our case, but quickly realized that we are genuinely interested and have the necessary knowledge. Then he quickly becomes friendly.

Francis and his daughter have at least five generations of predecessors in the vineyard and grape cultivation. He briefly outlines the family history: 'I'm from a family with three children. In 2009, we decided to each go our own way and the old champagne house Raymond Boulard ceased to exist. My sister stays in grape growing and my brother continues in his own way and does not follow the organic path I opted for. With my wife Jeanne and daughter Delphine, we founded the new champagne house Francis Boulard et Fille, with me representing the sixth generation. We found in the archives an ancestor born in 1792.'

Francis took his first steps in the vineyard behind the plough and the horse Bijou, together with grandfather Julien. Julien sold still wines and he resisted the rapid automation following the Second World War. In 1952, Francis' father Raymond came onto the estate and began to make champagne himself. Francis himself entered the business in 1970. With the knowledge of his grandfather and father, who also worked according to the seasons, Francis gave the big push to work more to biological principles.

Champagne
Francis Boulard & Fille
Route Nationale RD 944
F–51220 CAUROY-
LES-HERMONVILLE
+ 33 3 26 61 52 77
www.francis-boulard.com

In 1980, father Raymond Boulard died. In 2001, the decision was taken to stop using sprays and herbicides. Francis Boulard then went one step further and switched to biodynamic wine-growing. Biodynamics is a branch of organic viticulture, based on rejecting all chemical products and synthetic fertilizers. This means that the winegrower works in a natural way, based on the Steiner moon calendar, to promote energy flows and life in and on the soil. This improves the quality of the grapes. Francis works according to the moon calendar, just like his grandfather, an early proponent of biodynamic agriculture. The moon calendar indicates when is best to work the vineyard. We are working to the rhythm of nature and the seasons. This method became increasingly visible from 2000 onwards. In 2004, the champagne house received the Ecocert certificate and they aim to completely convert to biodynamic agriculture. For example, Francis has reduced the use of copper, which he calls a poison for the soil. Grass is allowed to grow between the vines to enrich the soil and reduce erosion. To counteract diseases, he protects the vines with, for example, hemp or sage, and he makes natural preparations that are pulverized in small amounts to strengthen the soil and increase the plants' resistance to disease.

→
François Boulard in his somewhat cramped, archaic cellar where chaos reigns

↓
In this barrel the malolactic fermentation is completed.

Attigny
VOU
PAUL FO
COLBERT
REIMS
CHAM
PA
GNE
1914-
Sillery
Verzonay
Verzy
Mailly   Mour-
Ay   melon
Bouzy
Mareuil
NAY
CHÂLONS
R. N. 3

Francis Boulard's vineyard is located partly in Cormicy, north-west of Reims, in the Massif de Saint-Thierry, also called La Petite Montagne. He also has plots in Paradis (Hameau de Belval in the Marne Valley), Cuchery, Cauroy-lès-Hermonville and Mailly-Champagne.

The soil consists of lime and flint. The vines are on average 45 years old. The best vines of a plot are used for replanting. In this way, the average quality, personality and character are retained. The vines are pruned short, to control yield and get a fuller taste. The grape bunches are rarely thinned.

Picking is followed by fine, delicate pressing. Vinification is by individual plot. Francis does not intervene during fermentation, but keeps a close eye on the initial fermentation that happens spontaneously with yeasts naturally present in the grape skins. The first fermentation takes place in large 2,000 litre *foudres*, in 500-600 litre *demi-muid* barrels or in 300 litre oak barrels. The wooden barrels originate from Burgundy or Champagne and are on average twelve years old. The oxygen control ensures smooth, round, yet mineral wines. The wines are stored on their fine lees. *Bâtonnage* takes place every twelve days to increase the complexity of the wine. The *bâtonnage* also depends on the variety of grapes available. Bottling and *dégorgement* take place on the estate.

During our visit, we were interrupted by a Belgian couple asking whether it would be possible to taste a glass of champagne. Francis explained that he was in the middle of a meeting and that they could buy a bottle to drink on the terrace. That's not what the visitors expected and they continued on their way. This was a perfect illustration of what Francis indicated at the beginning, and why he has become so distrustful. 'Every day we are confronted with this, people seem to think that a champagne house is a free café.' Too bad that the passers-by were Belgians. As countrymen we experience a sense of substitute shame.

Conclusion

Although the first acquaintance with Francis Boulard was a little difficult, after what turned into a four-hour visit we left as friends. We got to know Francis as a sensitive man who has suffered heavily from the divorce from his brother and sister. He would have liked things to have happened differently, but unfortunately they did not share his passion for biodynamic wine-growing.

CUVÉES AND MILLÉSIMÉS

LES MURGIERS, BLANC DE NOIRS

soil	clay and limestone soil
grape varieties	100% Pinot Meunier from on average 30-year-old vines
dosage	3 to 5 g/litre for the extra brut 0 g/litre for the brut nature
type	extra brut, brut nature
production	Only the first juice of the first pressing is used. The wine is vinified in small oak barrels, *foudres* and large old barrels (*demi-muids*). Malolactic fermentation and *bâtonnage*
results	The estate's first cuvée Blanc de Noirs, that is white wine from blue grapes

VIEILLES VIGNES, BLANC DE BLANCS

terroir	Le Murtet plot
soil	Lime and flint soil
grape varieties	100% Chardonnay
dosage	3 to 5 g/litre for the extra brut 0 g/litre for the brut nature
type	extra brut, brut nature

GRAND CRU GRANDE MONTAGNE (MAILLY-CHAMPAGNE)

classification	grand cru
terroir	Mailly-Champagne
soil	clay and limestone soil
grape varieties	60% Pinot Noir, 40% Chardonnay
dosage	3 to 5 g/liter for the extra brut 0 g/litre for the brut nature
type	extra brut, brut nature
production	The wine is vinified in small oak barrels and large barrels (*demi-muids*). 30% old reserve wines are used for assembly.
results	This champagne scores well in all guides.

ROSÉ DE SAIGNÉE

soil	clay and limestone soil
grape varieties	50% Pinot Noir, 50% Pinot Meunier from on average 40-year-old vines
dosage	5 g/litre for the extra brut 0 g/litre for the brut nature
type	extra brut, brut nature

MILLÉSIMÉ

terroir	Montagne de Reims and Marne Valley
soil	clay and limestone soil
grape varieties	30% Pinot Noir, 20% Pinot Meunier, 50% Chardonnay from on average 30-year-old vines
assembly	millésime
dosage	3 g/litre
type	extra brut
production	Only the first juice of the first pressing is used for this champagne.

Petraea

terroir	Vallée de la Marne and Montagne de Reims
soil	clay and limestone soil
grape varieties	60% Pinot Noir, 20% Pinot Meunier, 20% Chardonnay from on average 35-year-old vines
assembly	millésime
dosage	0 g/litre
type	brut nature
production	Only the first juice of the first pressing is used for this champagne. This champagne is made according to a system that looks very similar to the solera system: each year, wine from the latest grape harvest is added to the barrel so that one quarter of the barrel is new wine. In this way all previous years are present, but in ever smaller proportions (the older the wine, the less of it present). This 'perpetual' stock was launched in 1997.

Les Rachais

terroir	From the Massif de Saint-Thierry
soil	lime and flint soil
grape varieties	100% Chardonnay from on average 43-year-old vines
dosage	0 g/litre
type	brut nature
results	100% biodynamic, Ecocert certified

Les Rachais Rosé

terroir	From two plots in the Massif de Saint-Thierry
soil	lime and flint soil
grape varieties	100% Pinot Noir from on average 30-year-old vines
dosage	2 g/litre
type	extra brut
results	biodynamic, Ecocert certified

CHAMPAGNE J. VIGNIER

Nathalie Vignier:
'History repeats itself from generation to generation'

We are received by Nathalie Vignier at champagne house J. Vignier in Cramant. This is *the* grand cru region. Nathalie is the daughter of Jean Vignier and granddaughter of Paul Lebrun. The family has a long history in winegrowing, dating back to 1530 and Nathalie is happy to tell us that 'Nicolas Vignier lived in Bar-sur-Seine and

was connected to the court of Henri III. My great-grandfather, the father of my grandmother Marie Louise Lebrun, was active in agriculture in Saudoy and had a passion for viticulture. When he died during the First World War, his son distributed the property, keeping the best farmland for himself, and leaving his sister the steep slopes in Cramant. When those slopes were later classified as *appellation Grand Cru*, there was a break in the family.'

Since Nathalie's grandfather Paul Lebrun had only daughters, her mother was the last Lebrun. For this reason, the name of the house was adapted to that of Nathalie's father, Jean Vignier, and became Maison Vignier-Lebrun.

During the Second World War, a friendship blossomed between grandfather Paul Lebrun and a German prisoner. Even after the war, the German regularly returned to Cramant. Today, the man's great-nephew, Sebastian Nickel, is co-founder of the Champagne

J. Vignier project. Nathalie: 'By 'our project', we mean we are sober winegrowers. We only use grapes from our own vineyards. We work on a plot-by-plot basis. We opt for tasty, healthy grapes and make a strict selection. As a result, we have a limited return. The use of herbicides is out. We vinify in stainless steel to preserve the purity of the fruit. All wines undergo malolactic fermentation to promote the aromatic variety.'

Récoltant manipulant

25,000 bottles

Champagne J. Vignier

427 rue de la Libération

F–51530 CRAMANT

+ 33 6 84 77 33 32

www.champagnevignier.fr

Nathalie is now the tenth generation in winegrowing and the sixth in the grand cru village of Cramant. Initially, she did not want to continue her parents' work, but fate decided otherwise. But since then, she has come to realize how fascinating this work is. Her little son is two years old and today there is a crane in front of the house for

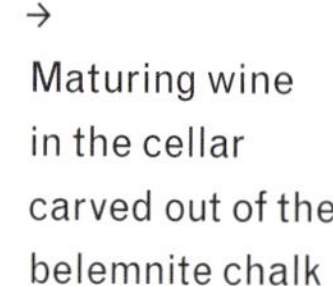

building a new cellar. 'When I was two years old, there was also a crane', Nathalie tells us. 'My father was also building a new barrel cellar at the time. In this way, history repeats itself and the generations succeed one another.'

The plots of the Champagne house J. Vignier are located mainly on the Côte des Blancs, in Cramant, Chouilly and Oiry, three of the seventeen classified grand cru villages.

All the vines in Cramant, Chouilly and Oiry were planted between 1950 and 2010 and rooted deep into a chalk layer.

The house wants to reflect in its champagne the unique character of the terroir, and the harmony between the soil, the climate and the Chardonnay grapes.

J. Vignier also has plots on the Coteaux du Sézannais, 50 km to the south, where the climate is milder. They have transferred the best Cramant vines to these plots. The combination of the rich soil, the warmer climate and these vines produces an unusual champagne. On the chalk soil, you will find little bits of flint and carnelian. These warm up in the sun during the day and return the warmth to the soil in the evening.

Pressing is done in Cramant only, with, until 2008, around 140,000 bottles a year turned by hand. When their *remueur* retired in 2008, they switched to a mechanical system.

The house has four different cuvées.

Conclusion

The family motto is *'La bonté de l'esprit et la grandeur de courage'* or 'The goodness of the spirit and the greatness of courage'.

Champagne J. Vignier is a sub-project for plot wines within the traditional Vignier Lebrun house, delivering champagne of unprecedented finesse. The house continues to produce Champagne Paul Lebrun, aimed at a loyal, traditional customer base. The J. Vignier champagne was a nice surprise for us.

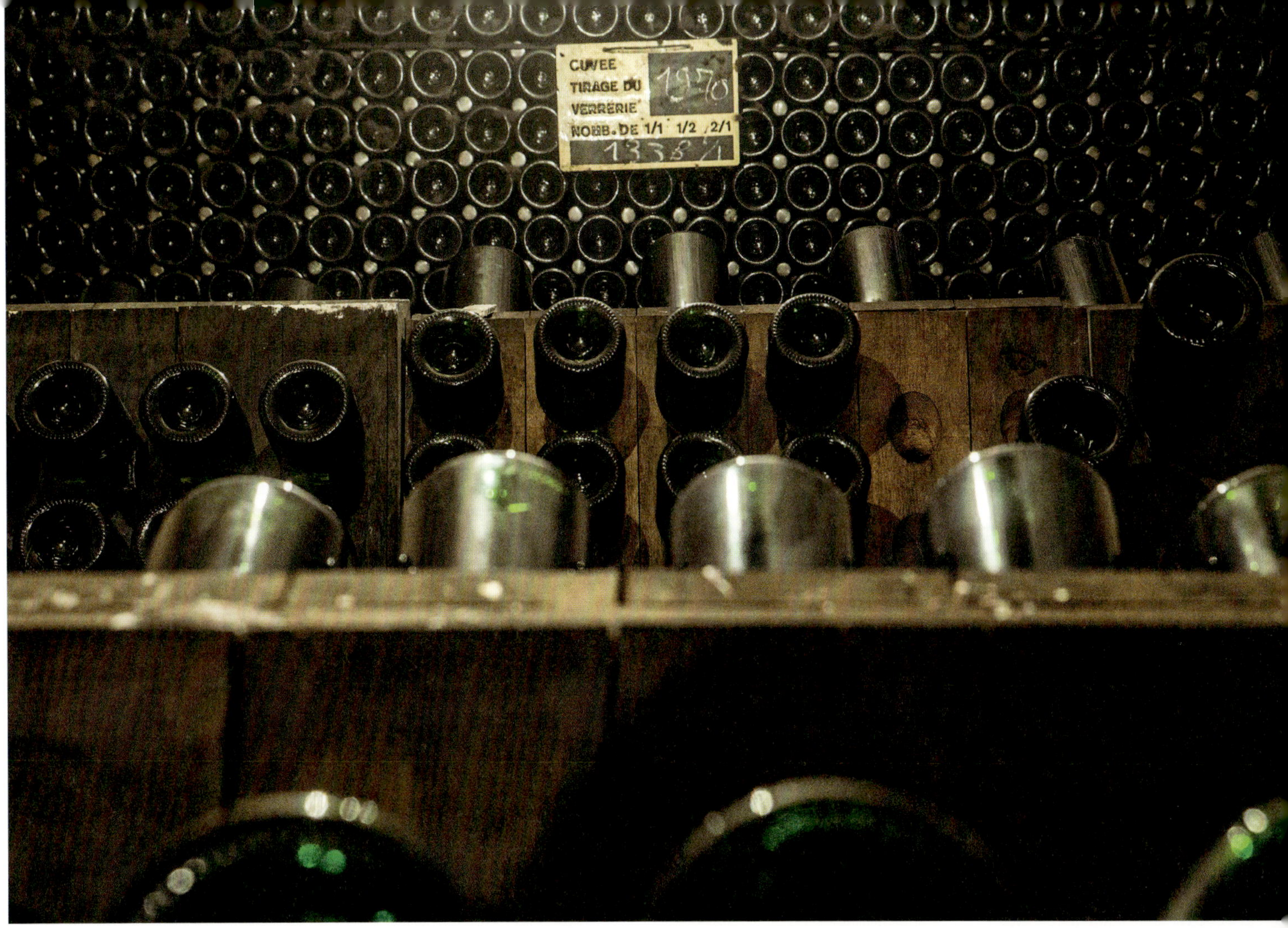
CUVEE
TIRAGE DU
VERRERIE
NOBB. DE 1/1 1/2 2/1

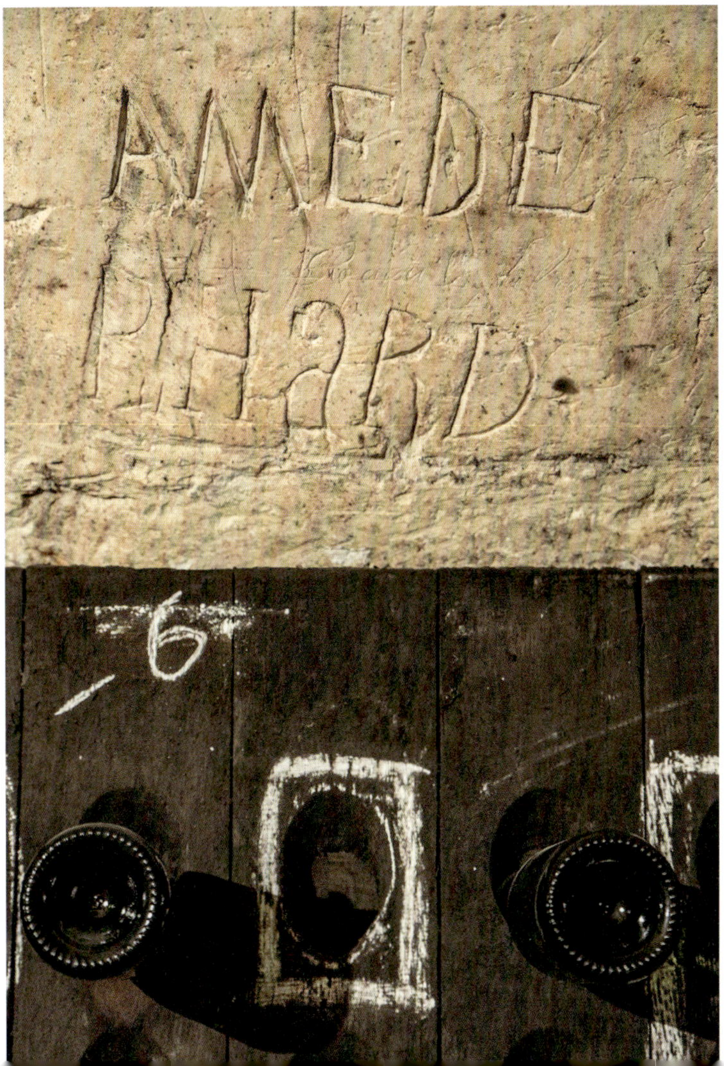
AMEDE

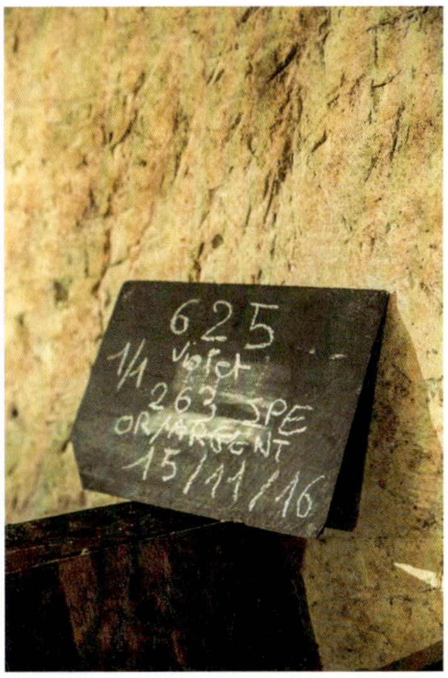
625

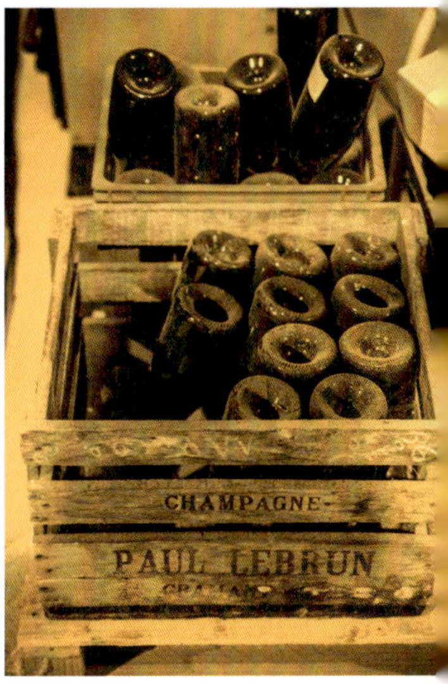
CHAMPAGNE
PAUL LEBRUN

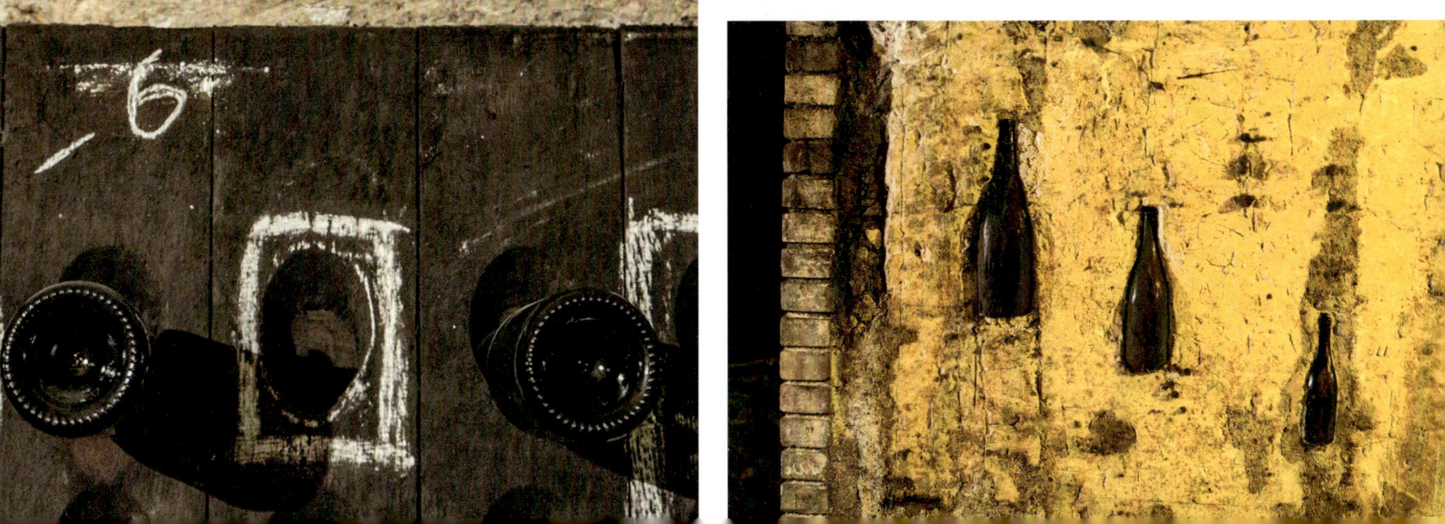

←
Transition
from the new
concrete
basement to
the traditional,
belemnite chalk
cellar

↗
Ripening in
wooden barrels
and storage
sur pointe

CUVÉES AND MILLÉSIMÉS

Ora Alba

classification	grand cru
terroir	from plots in Chouilly, Oiry and Cramant
soil	chalk soil
grape varieties	100% Chardonnay
assembly	assembly of grand crus, 70% millésime of 2009 and 30% of 2010 and 2011
dosage	5 g/litre
type	brut
production	kept five years *sur lies*

Silexus Sezannensis

terroir	Le Chatet plot, in Saudoy
soil	flinty topsoil, chalky subsoil
grape varieties	100% Chardonnay
assembly	millésime of 2011
dosage	5 g/litre
type	brut
production	stored four years before *dégorgement*, kept five years *sur lies*

Les Longues Verges

classification	grand cru
terroir	The name refers to the plot located at Cramant and Chouilly.
soil	chalk soil
grape varieties	100% Chardonnay
assembly	millésime of 2013
dosage	5 g/litre
type	brut
production	kept four years *sur lies*

Champagne J. Vignier

terroir	originating from a plot in Cramant and a plot in Barbonne Fayel (Coteaux du Sézannais)
soil	chalk soil
grape varieties	100% Chardonnay
assembly	2008
dosage	5 g/litre
type	brut
production	kept eight years *sur lies*

CHAMPAGNE
Françoise Bedel
Domaine cultivé en Bio-Dynamie
Tél 03 23 82 15 80
Horaires d'ouverture :
Du lundi au vendredi
de 9ʰ à 12ʰ30 et de 13ʰ30 à 18ʰ
Week-ends et jours fériés
sur rendez-vous
CHAMPAGNE
F. BEDEL
PROPRIÉTAIRE-RÉCOLTANT
Crouttes ★ Marne
vigneron
indépendant

CHAMPAGNE FRANÇOISE BEDEL ET FILS

Françoise Bedel, queen of Pinot Meunier

Champagne Françoise Bedel et Fils is a third-generation house of winegrowers with a domain located near Château-Thierry, between Paris and Reims. The company is headed by a woman, Françoise Bedel. Though not the most welcoming individual, we nevertheless want to meet her, as this is a top house for biodynamic viticulture.

The 8.4-hectare estate produces some 70,000 bottles a year, with the grapes coming from vines on average between 30 and 60 years old. Located in Crouttes-sur-Marne, Nanteuil-sur-Marne, Charly-sur-Marne and Villiers-Saint-Denis, the plots all have a clay-limestone soil.

'We are constantly searching for harmony and balance between the vineyard and the wine', says Françoise Bedel, explaining how and when she converted to biodynamics. 'My son Vincent was born in 1980, but in 1982 he started getting health problems. I got to know a couple of homeopathic physicians and this broadened my horizon.'

She had her first contact with biodynamics in 1996, and one year later stopped using pesticides and started working the soil with a plough only. In 1998, two hectares were converted to biodynamics, followed by a further seven hectares in 1999. All now have Ecocert certification. By 2006, all plots had been converted to biodynamic viticulture.

Champagne

Françoise Bedel et Fils

71, Grande Rue

F–02310 CROUTTES-

SUR-MARNE

+ 33 3 23 82 15 80

www.champagne-bedel.fr

First appearing in 1924, biodynamics was the brainchild of Rudolf Steiner. The founder of anthroposophy, he was convinced that anyone eating inferior-quality food would feel bad. Working with a few pioneering farmers and after eight conferences, a new way of farming – published in English as 'The Agriculture Course' – was developed by Steiner, based on the following principles:

> Soil and plant fertilization using preparations derived from plants, livestock and minerals.
> Application of these preparations at the right time, in line with the vegetation cycle and in accordance with the moon and planetary calendar.
> Working the soil through ploughing and raking.

Françoise Bedel: 'Biodynamic agriculture basically means taking care of the soil, ensuring its balance for the benefit of the crops, in harmony with the soil and its environment. In our case, this is all about promoting exchange between the soil and the vineyard's root system, ultimately allowing the full expression of the soil in the grapes. This is very important for me. All grapes are harvested by hand by the same team we've been using for the last 20 years.'

The three grape varieties (pinot meunier, pinot noir et chardonnay) are pressed separately, plot by plot, using a pneumatic press. The juice must not come into contact with the stalks.

The goal is to create a perfect wine. It is matured in oak barrels, giving richness and a beautiful aroma to the wine. Bottling is done in line with the Maria Thun moon calendar. 'The compost, which has a major influence on plant propagation, is spread in autumn. The soil wakes up at the autumn equinox on 21 September and goes back to sleep at the spring equinox on 21 March. 'It is during this time that the soil is supplied with oxygen and bacterial life is promoted. Raking, turning up and treading down the soil promote the activity of the many micro-organisms present in it. Without such activity, you'll never manage to get the full effect of the terroir', Bedel went on to say.

↓
Champagne corks fastened with hempen string and typical sealing wax

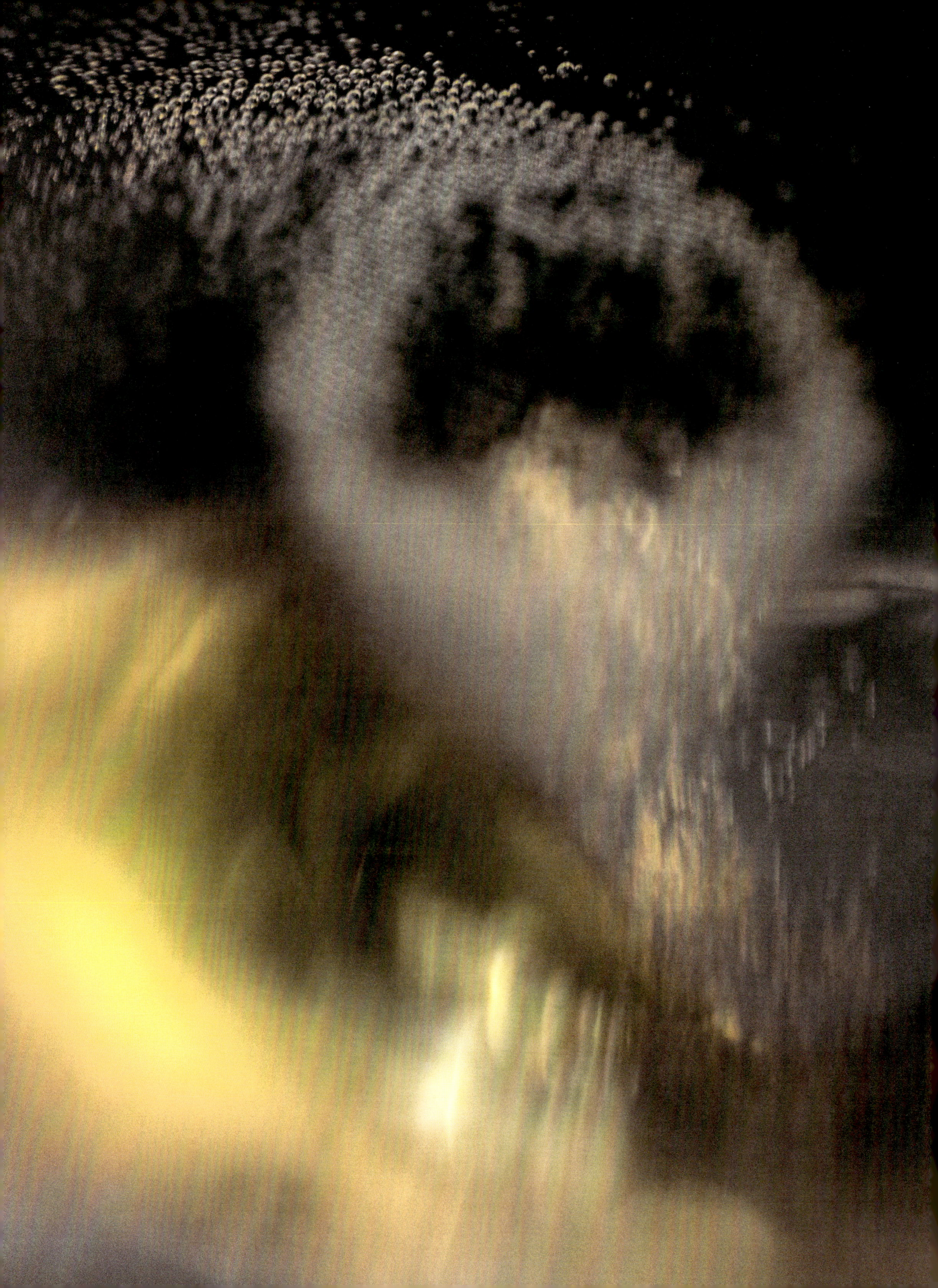

'Following years of research, Maria Thun found out that the cosmos has a major influence on plants. The sun, the moon and all other planets influence plants, livestock and humans in different ways.'

The timing of the tastings that take place on the domain at the end of October are also determined by the Maria Thun moon calendar. All champagnes are tasted blind and the domain produces champagne brut nature, brut and extra brut.

Conclusion A top house for biodynamic viticulture, run under the motto of Antoine de Saint-Exupéry: 'We don't inherit the ground from our forefathers, we borrow it from our children'.

← Filling and 'dressing' (corking) the bottle

↓ The *cuvées* of the Bedel house

CUVÉES AND MILLÉSIMÉS

ORIGIN'ELLE

soil	clay, loam and marl on a limestone substrate
grape varieties	10% Pinot Noir, 75% Pinot Meunier, 15% Chardonnay
results	expression of Pinot Meunier, round and fresh

DIS 'VIN SECRET'

soil	loam and marl on a limestone substrate
grape varieties	8% Pinot Noir, 86% Pinot Meunier, 6% Chardonnay

ENTRE CIEL ET TERRE

soil	mainly clay and marl on a limestone substrate
grape varieties	100% Pinot Meunier

L'ÂME DE LA TERRE

soil	clay, loam and marl on a limestone substrate
grape varieties	17% Pinot Noir, 67% Pinot Meunier, 16% Chardonnay
assembly	millésimé

COMME AUTREFOIS

soil	clay, loam and marl on a limestone substrate
grape varieties	40% Pinot Noir, 40% Pinot Meunier, 20% Chardonnay
type	extra brut
production	stored under cork, matured in barrels for 12 years, vinified in oak barrels

ROBERT WINER MILLÉSIME 1996

grape varieties	6% Pinot Noir, 88% Pinot Meunier, 6% Chardonnay
assembly	millésimé
production	This champagne is stored under cork, vinified in enamel vats and matured for 14 years *sur lies*.
results	This champagne is a homage to Robert Winner, their friend and homeopathic physician.

CHAMPAGNE
Chartogne-Taillet

CHAMPAGNE CHARTOGNE-TAILLET

Alexandre Taillet:
'You can deceive your wife, but not a customer'

Some 8 km from Reims, on the southern edge of the Massif de Saint-Thierry, we stopped by the Chartogne-Taillet domain in Merfy, where we were welcomed by Alexandre Taillet. He is a *récoltant-manipulant* and works to the motto: small yields, top quality.

The family history tells us that this house was already growing wine in 1485 in Merfy. Everything started with Fiacre Taillet and the same blood still flows through the veins of this champagne house.

Alexandre worked previously in Burgundy, and was once an apprentice of Anselme Selosse. He runs the vineyard in a totally biodynamic manner, aiming to produce 100,000 bottles a year on his 11 hectares spread out over Merfy, Chenay and Saint-Thierry. The house possesses old vines without a rootstock.

A few years ago, Alexandre started dividing up the various plots as done in the 17th century, following the old land registry maps found in the impressive family archives with its collection of diaries. It was customary for all family members to keep a diary, and these diaries speak not just about wine-growing, but also about culture and politics. Even Alexandre's small son, Hélois, already has his own diary.

For instance, the diary kept by Antoine Taillet notes the following: 'It's the 2nd of July 1812 and the weather is much too cold. The grapes are falling off and the cold spell is expected to last until the 16th of July. We're in for a storm, but then things will get better.'

The family attaches great importance to its history, and in some fields old habits live on.

Alexandre tells us about his passion for working the complex soil. The many micro-organisms present in the soil add to the value of the terroir and to the quality of the grapes. Great care is needed to protect this fragile equilibrium.

Champagne Chartogne-Taillet
37-39, Grande Rue
F–51220 MERFY
+ 33 3 26 03 10 17
www.chartogne-taillet.com

'As a winegrower,' Alexandre says, 'it's my responsibility to make optimal use of this. Every year, Claude and Lydia Bourguignon analyse the health of fauna and flora on the domain. The Bourguignons are the leading experts in geology and soil analysis in the wine world.'

The goal is for each plant to be able to fully express itself. For instance, Alexandre will never compact the soil too hard, and he refuses to allow a tractor into the vineyard. Instead he uses horses, thereby allowing more oxygen to get into the soil. All chemical herbicides are banned and he uses hundreds of local herbs to ensure soil health in a natural manner. Alexandre is no fan of machines. 'Machines can replace men, but they have a negative influence on the wine', he finds. 'When you don't use machines, people spend more time in the vineyard, and are thus in much closer harmony with nature.' Once harvested, the grapes get pressed as quickly as possible to gain the best quality juice.

Conclusion   Vibrant champagnes, a piece of history in the hands of a new top generation.

 Champagne Chartogne-Taillet

← ←
Alexandre Taillet
lets us taste his
champagne in
the historical
cellar of the
Chartogne-
Taillet family

←
Visibly this
champagne is
still unfiltered

↑
Champagne
maturing *sur
lattes* and
on *pupitres*

↓
The packaging
line, one of the
few pieces of
mechanical
equipment in
the Chartogne-
Taillet house

→
The family
library with an
old land registry
map Alexandre
uses for dividing
up his plots

↓
When opening,
the bottle is
held at an angle
to avoid losing
the wine

CUVÉES AND MILLÉSIMÉS

Cuvée Sainte Anne

terroir	the Les Beaux Sens plot in Merfy
soil	sand, clay and limestone
grape varieties	Pinot Noir, Pinot Meunier and Chardonnay From vines on average 25 years old
assembly	Dependent on the vintage
dosage	4.5-7 g/litre
type	extra brut, brut
production	Vinified in stainless steel tanks, no filtration, natural yeasts
results	The cuvées have all the typical properties of the soil found in Merfy,

Rosé

soil	Sand and limestone
grape varieties	The cépages are dependent on the year of harvesting; no Pinot Meunier is used in this cuvée.
assembly	millésimé
dosage	5.5 g/litre
type	brut
production	Vinified in stainless steel tanks, no filtration, natural yeasts. The red wine used to make the rosé comes from the Les Orizeaux plot (Pinot Noir grapes).

Millésime

terroir	Les Couarres, a plot in the middle of Merfy
soil	clay
grape varieties	60% Pinot Noir, 40% Chardonnay From 30-year-old vines
assembly	millésimé
dosage	6 g/litre
production	Vinified in stainless steel tanks, and stored *sur lies* until March of the following year.
results	a beautiful, deep, rich and yet mineral taste. It is one of the domain's top champagnes.

Fiacre

terroir	From 2 plots close to each other: Le Chemin de Reims and Les Orizeaux
soil	Sand with limestone
grape varieties	40% Pinot Noir, 60% Chardonnay
assembly	millésimé
dosage	6-7 g/litre
type	brut
production	Vinified in stainless steel tanks, just the *tête de cuvée* is used.
results	a champagne with precision and great finesse.

Les Barres

terroir	the Les Barres plot in Merfy
soil	A sandy soil with less limestone than in the other plots. The limestone is deeper down.
grape varieties	100% Pinot Meunier The Pinot Meunier grapes come from one of the rare vineyards with untouched vines. The vines are 60 years old. They are planted on sandy soil where phylloxera has no chance.
assembly	millésimé
dosage	0 g/litre
type	extra brut
production	Vinified in 3-9 year-old barrels, no filtration, natural yeasts

Les Alliées

terroir	the Les Alliées plot, a bit further away than the other plots
soil	sandy
grape varieties	100% Pinot Meunier The vines were planted in 1969.
assembly	millésimé
dosage	3 g/litre
type	extra brut
production	spontaneous fermentation, no filtration
results	an extra brut with a pleasing acidity

Les Orizeaux

terroir	the Les Orizeaux plot in Merfy
soil	Sand with chalk
grape varieties	100% Pinot Noir From vines more than 50 years old
assembly	millésimé
dosage	0 g/litre
type	extra brut
production	Vinified in 3-9 year-old barrels no filtration, natural yeasts
results	Though the vines stand on sandy soil, you can taste the silt coming off the rock below. An elegant champagne.

Heurtebise, Blanc de Blancs

terroir	the Les Heurtebise plot in Merfy
soil	Sand with limestone
grape varieties	100% Chardonnay From vines on average 35 years old
assembly	millésimé
dosage	Dependent on the vintage
type	brut
production	Vinified in stainless steel vats, no filtration, natural yeasts

CHAMPAGNE JÉRÔME PRÉVOST

**Jérôme Prévost is always
on the lookout for new things**

In 1987, Jérôme Prévost inherited 2 hectares from his grandmother. Of Polish origin, she rented out her vines. 'The two hectares represented her old-age pension', said Jérôme. 'On inheriting from her in 1987, I first sold the grapes to a *négociant*. It was my good friend Anselme Selosse who got me making wine myself. But I didn't have anything, not even cellars. It took Anselme proposing to give up a corner of his cellar to convince me. In 2002, I found a location in Gueux.'

We met up with Jérôme in Gueux. Anselme helped and supported him for 24 seasons. In 2003, the whole production moved to Gueux. Jérôme owns two hectares planted with old Pinot Meunier vines, all of which came from the same vineyard, Les Béguines in Gueux. This vineyard has a density of 8,300 to 10,000 vines per hectare and has a north-south orientation. Use of insecticides was stopped in 1994, followed by herbicides in 1996. In 2000, mycorrhization (the coupling of a plant with a mushroom or fungus) was introduced.

In addition, he owns around 20 ares adjacent to Les Béguines, planted with Pinot Meunier, Pinot Blanc, Pinot Noir and Chardonnay. The vines are still very young and their grapes are blended with the Pinot Meunier.

The vineyards are located to the west of Reims. The sandy soil has traces of limestone which are over 55 million years old and the presence of fossils provides the wines with their mineral taste.

Jérôme makes one wine from a single vineyard and just Pinot Meunier (apart from the other 20 ares in Les Béguines). Winemaking is done as naturally as the winegrowing. For Jérôme, the emphasis is on the wine, and not so much on the cellar. 'The most important thing is that the grapes are ripe.'

Champagne Jérôme Prévost

Récoltant manipulant

2, rue de la Petite Montagne

F–51390 GUEUX

+ 33 3 26 03 48 60

www.champagnelacloserie.fr

No pesticides or herbicides are used. Picking is done by hand and pressing by gravity. There is no chaptalisation, and vinification takes place in barrels. Fermentation is spontaneous and bottling is done late, sometime around June and using a minimum of sulphur. There is no cold stabilisation, no filtration. All bottles are disgorged at once. The wine is matured for 3 years *sur lattes*.

The two cuvées are 'La closerie Les Béguines extra brut' and 'Fac similé rosé'. 'The rosé came first', he confessed, 'because I dreamt of making a red wine.' For him, making red wine is more fun than making white wine. 'The only reason is that the best flavour of the grape is in the skin. But in champagne, you press the grapes quickly to prevent the red colour.'

Full of curiosity, Jérôme is always on the lookout for new things. 'I have this from my father', he says, 'but it is also necessary. Because curiosity not only causes doubt, but also sometimes ecstatic joy when working on the slopes, sometimes even putting you into a trance. I'm very demanding, but also intuitive, something I got from my mother.'

Conclusion With the house producing just 13,000 bottles a year, we can refer to this as a demanding mini-project.

ICI, C'EST DÉJA LA VITICULTURE DE DEUX MAINS

« SI VOUS AVEZ UN PROBLÈME AVEC LA QUALITÉ, ESSAYEZ LA QUANTITÉ. »

CUVÉES AND MILLÉSIMÉS

La Closerie Les Béguines extra brut

terroir	From the hamlet of Les Béguines (literally a 'bundle of vines'). A *closerie* is an estate or farm 2-3 hectares in size.
soil	Located at an altitude of 120 metres, the vineyard has a sandy limestone soil, dating back to the Palaeocene epoch.
grape varieties	2% Pinot Noir, 94% Pinot Meunier, 2% Chardonnay, 2% Pinot Gris
dosage	2.5 g/litre
type	extra brut
production	The wine undergoes malolactic fermentation, and no machinery or electricity is used in bottling. The wine is stored in 225-600 litre wooden barrels.

Fac Similé, assemblage-rosé

terroir	Les Béguines
assembly	87% basis wine from Les Béguines, 13% still red wine from Les Béguines, also Pinot Meunier
dosage	2-3 g/litre
type	extra brut
result	Just 3,300 bottles of this champagne are produced each year.

←
For Jacques Prévost, champagne is winemaking poetry

CHAMPAGNE DE SOUSA

Today we are at champagne house De Sousa in Avize, Côte des Blancs, where we are welcomed by Charlotte de Sousa, a charming young lady in charge of the domain under the strict supervision of her father Erick.

The family history goes back to the First World War. Among the Allies were Portuguese soldiers, some of the many soldiers nicknamed 'Les Poilus' (literally the 'hairy ones', as they often had difficulty getting their hair and beards cut in the trenches).

Born near to Porto, Manuel de Sousa was one of them. After the war, he returned to Portugal. During his absence, however, his business had floundered and he found it difficult to get back on his feet again. This led to his decision to return to France. Together with his wife and baby Antoine, they moved to Avize. Manuel had to work hard as a hired manual labourer. Every day would see him bringing iron-rich earth from the woods to the vineyard by horse and cart. But fate stepped in, with Manuel dying of a brain tumour at the early age of 29, leaving behind his wife and child.

A few years later, Antoine, now a young man, got to know Zoémie Bonneville from the Bonnevilles, a family with a generations-old tradition of winemaking. His marriage to Zoémie formed the basis of the success story of what was to become the De Sousa champagne house. In 1986, Antoine's son, Erick de Sousa (Charlotte's father) took over the domain from his father, running it together with his wife Michelle. They live to the rhythm of the seasons, sharing the adventure and their passion for champagne. Their three children, Charlotte, Julie and Valentin are being prepared to carry on the work, with all three receiving training in winegrowing.

While Julie is still studying, Charlotte and Valentin already work full-time at the domain.

Champagne De Sousa

Négociant manipulant

12, place Léon Bourgeois

F–51190 AVIZE

+ 33 3 26 57 53 29

www.champagnedesousa.com

The secret of the De Sousa house is that it works with old, deep-rooted vines. The deeper the roots plunge, the more the taste of the terroir gets into the grapes. This is exactly what De Sousa is striving for: the full expression of the terroir in its champagne. As the roots reach down very deep, fertilisers have difficulty getting down to them.

In 2010, the house switched to being fully organic and was awarded its bio-certificate in 2013. De Sousa produces 100,000 bottles a year on 42 plots spread over 11 hectares of chalky soil. 30% of the vines are Pinot Noir, 10% Pinot Meunier and 60% Chardonnay. 70% of the old vines are on average 45 years old. Density is 8,000 vines per hectare. The Chablis and Cordon de Royat pruning methods are used.

The one drawback we noticed during our visit is that the domain is located in the middle of Avize in two separate buildings, making handling difficult. The house had just taken delivery of a new press when we arrived. Classical music reverberates in the rooms where the wine is stored. On remarking that this was nice for the staff, Erick de Sousa corrected me, saying that the music 'is not for the staff but for the wine'. Of note are the crystal glass accessories between the barrels. According to Erick de Sousa, crystal glass boosts the wine's energy value.

Also noteworthy is the *cuve ovoïde*, an egg-shaped vat made entirely of wood. This helps regulate the oxygen, Erick explained to us. Vinification takes place in enamel vats, giving the wine a better balance. The cellar temperature is kept at a constant 10°C and *remuage* (turning the filled bottles) is still done by hand. There's always something going on in this house.

Conclusion   This is a strict, well-structured house driven by the will to constantly do better.

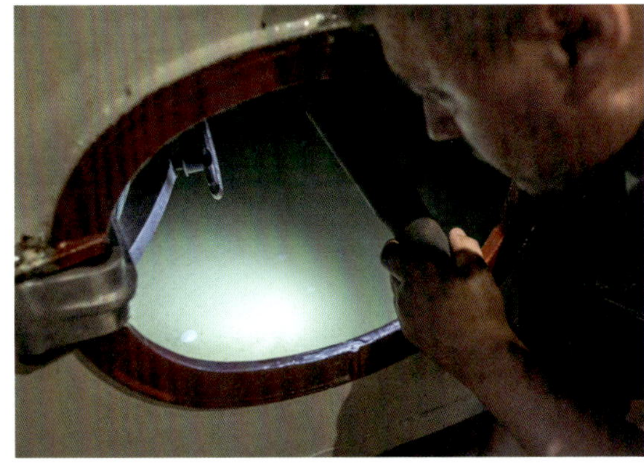

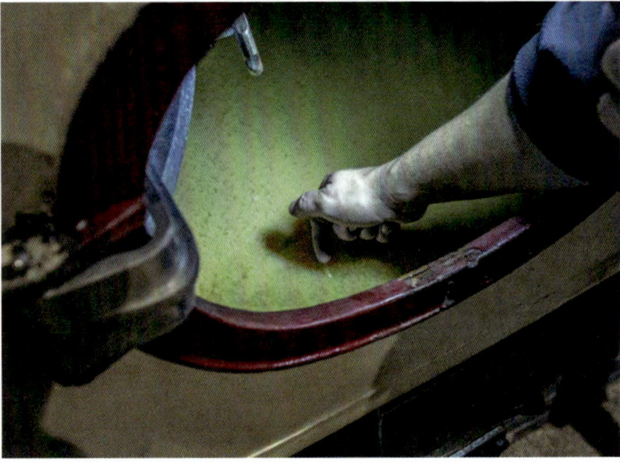

↑
Sous-tirage
to remove excess
thick yeasts and
impurities

↗
Oval-shaped
wooden tank,
example of an
experiment in
biodynamic
convection

⇒
Champagne is
stored in wooden
barrels but is
also vinified in
enamelled tanks

→
Charlotte de
Sousa manages
the De Sousa
champagne house
with her father Erick

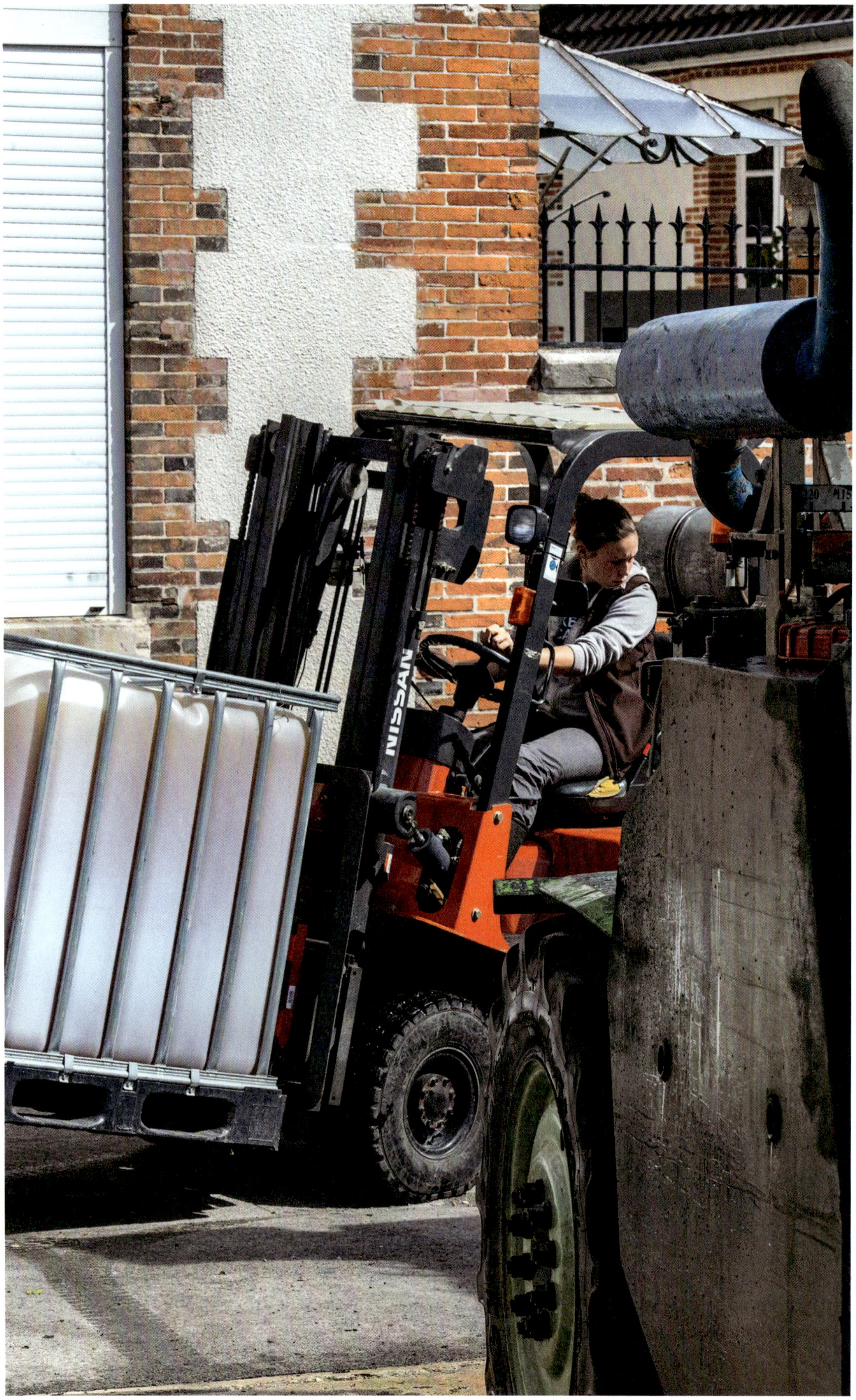
NISSAN

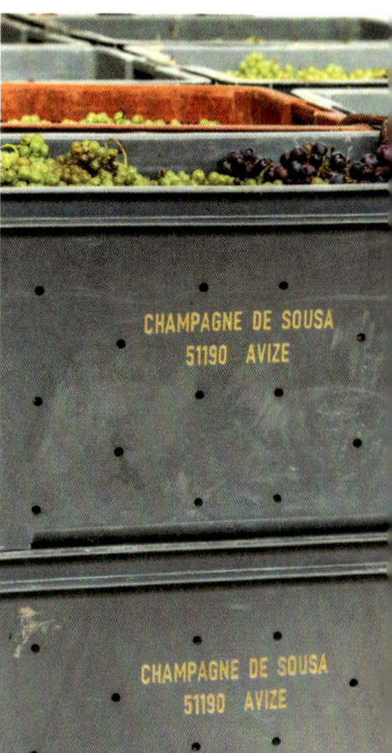

CHAMPAGNE DE SOUSA
51190 AVIZE
CHAMPAGNE DE SOUSA
51190 AVIZE

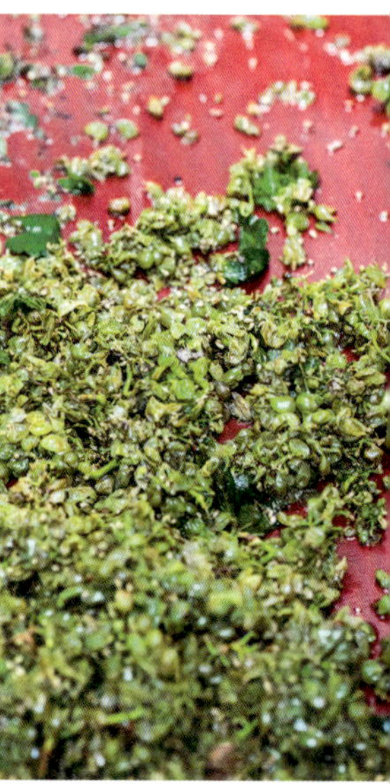

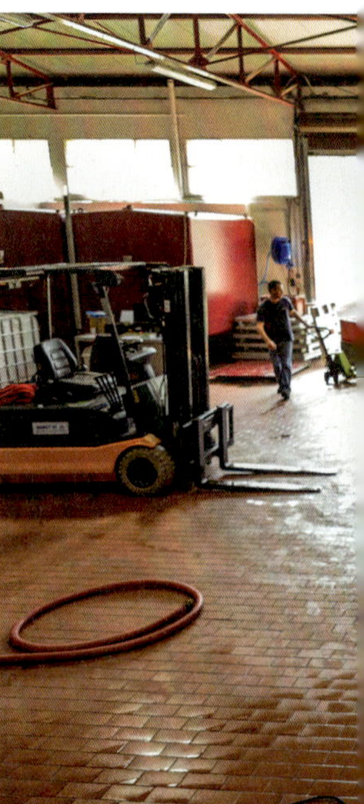

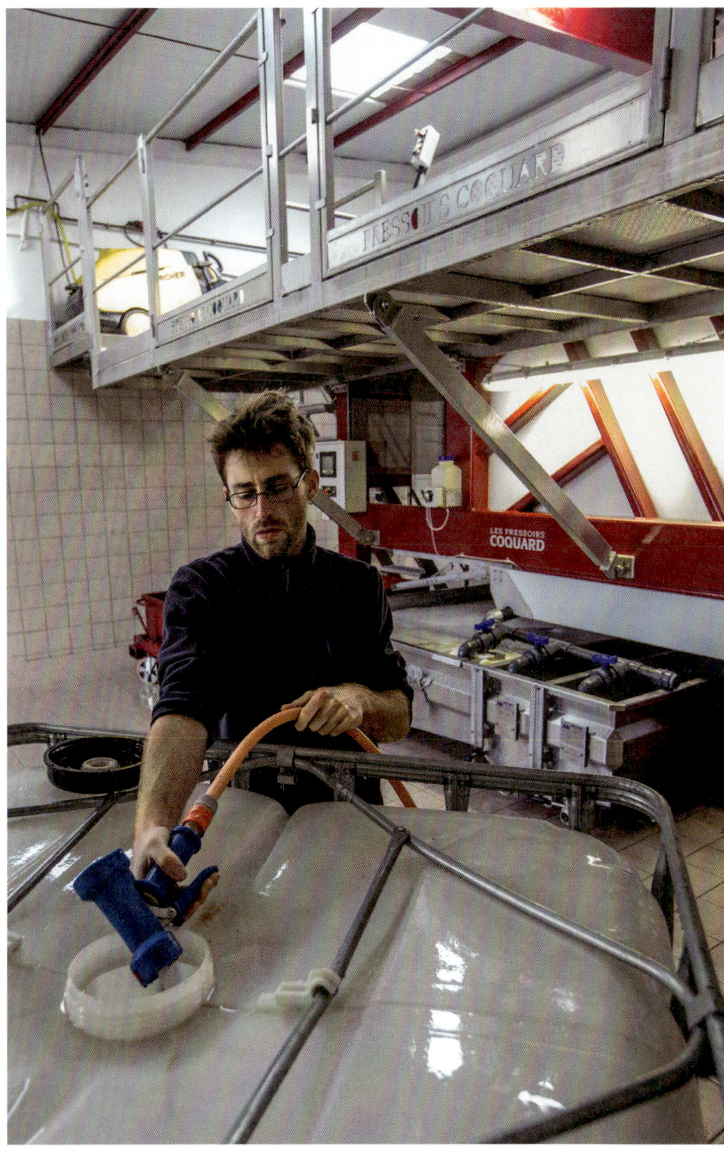

←← Charlotte likes to roll up her sleeves during harvesting

↑ Detail of the cutting and deleafing machine

→ Cleanliness is a high priority in the winery

↙ Detail of the Coquard à *plateau incliné* (lateral) press

← All hands on deck at harvest-time, here the grapes are being brought in and stripped from their stalks

↓ Bringing in the grapes. The pressed juice is put into transit tanks.

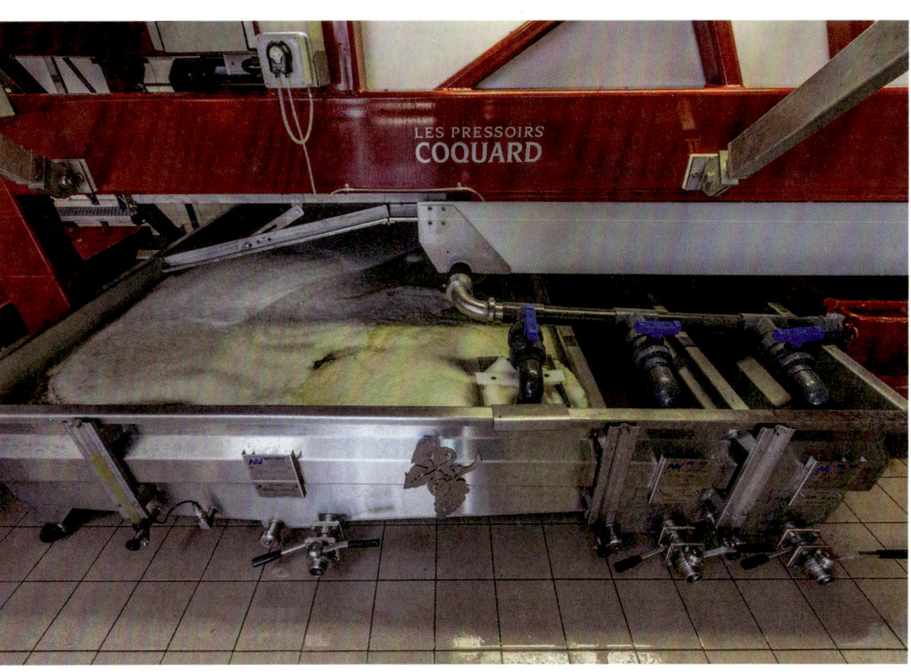

CUVÉES AND MILLÉSIMÉS

BLANC DE NOIRS

classification	grand cru
terroir	After mulling it over for years, Erick and his family decided to take on a new challenge, working with some Pinot Noir from the plots in Bouzy and Tours-sur-Marne, two historic grand cru villages in the Montagne de Reims.
grape varieties	100% Pinot Noir
dosage	7 g/litre
type	brut
production	Just 3,900 bottles are produced each year. The first cuvée was produced in 2012, stored for 10 months on wood and bottled in 2013. Fermentation is spontaneous and there is no filtration. *Bâtonnage* (stirring the settled lees back into the wine) in the barrels is practised, as is *poignettage* (shaking the bottles) in the cellar. Stability is reached in the cellar 8 months after *dégorgement*. The Pinot Noir spends three years maturing in the cellars to ensure quality.

BRUT TRADITION

terroir	From Avize grand cru, Grauves premier cru and Mardeuil.
grape varieties	40% Pinot Noir, 10% Pinot Meunier, 50% Chardonnay
assembly	assembly of various vintages
type	brut
production	Fermentation is thermo-regulated. The grapes all come from the De Sousa vineyard and are picked when perfectly ripe.
results	The Pinot Noir gives the champagne its *rondeur*, the Pinot Meunier its taste of wine and the Chardonnay its finesse.

BRUT RÉSERVE, BLANC DE BLANCS

classification	grand cru
terroir	From grand cru plots in Avize, Cramant, Le Mesnil-sur-Oger and Oger.
grape varieties	100% Chardonnay, Chablis pruning
assembly	assembly of 2-3 vintages with at least 25% reserve wine
type	brut
production	Vinified in vats to maintain authenticity.

BRUT ROSÉ, ASSEMBLAGE-ROSÉ

classification	grand cru, premier cru
terroir	The Chardonnay grapes come from a plot in Grauve, the Pinot Noir from Aÿ.
grape varieties	10% Pinot Noir, 90% Chardonnay
type	brut

3A

classification	grand cru
terroir	The grapes come from 3 villages, all with names beginning with A: Aÿ, Avize and Ambonnay. The Chardonnay grapes come from Avize, in the Côte des Blancs. Half of the Pinot Noir grapes come from Aÿ, a village on the border between the Montagne de Reims and the Vallée de la Marne. South-facing slopes ensure that the Pinot Noir grapes get the most of the sun, giving them their finesse. The other half of the Pinot Noir grapes come from Ambonnay, also a grand cru village on the Montagne de Reims. Montagne de Reims is a long wooded plateau with a chalky soil, bordered by vineyards intentionally producing small yields since 1950.
soil	Chalk with a substrate of shell fossils
grape varieties	50% Pinot Noir, 50% Chardonnay From vines on average 50 years old.
production	The wine is matured is 250-litre barrels.
results	The chalk soil with its substrate of shell fossils gives the Chardonnay a beautiful finesse. This is our favourite.

Cuvée des Caudalies, Blanc de Blancs

classification	grand cru
terroir	Plots in Avize and Oger
grape varieties	100% Chardonnay
	From vines on average 50 years old
dosage	Less than 5 g/litre
type	extra brut
production	Everything is harvested by hand.
	The house has opted for a late harvest to get richly perfumed grapes.
	The champagne is 100% matured in barrels, 15% of which are new.
results	A family adventure goes with this champagne, a lovely mix of respect, pride, tradition and passion.
	'La Caudalie' is a unit used to measure a wine's expression, one *Caudalie* is equal to one second.

Cuvée des Caudalies grand cru

classification	grand cru
grape varieties	100% Chardonnay
	from vines on average 50 years old
assembly	millésimé
type	extra brut
production	To make this champagne, the best juice from the best vines is selected. The wine is vinified for ten months in wooden barrels. Fermentation is spontaneous, and the wine is not filtered. *Bâtonnage* in the barrel and *poignettage* (shaking the bottles) is done in the cellar (twice). Stability is achieved in the cellar after 12 months' *dégorgement*. The wine matures for more than seven years in the cellar.
results	According to Erick de Sousa, this champagne has a potential of 15-20 years.

Cuvée des Caudalies Rosé

classification	grand cru
grape varieties	10% Pinot Noir, 90% Chardonnay
type	brut
production	This cuvée is vinified in small barrels.

Umami

classification	grand cru
terroir	The grapes come from various grand cru plots belonging to the De Sousa house.
results	Umami is one of the five basic tastes, alongside salty, sour, sweet and bitter.
	When you taste this champagne, you also get a taste of depth, texture, reliëf, *rondeur*, vitality and minerality. In one word: the 'Umami' taste.

Mycorrhize

classification	grand cru
terroir	The grapes come from various plots. Biodynamic viticulture has been practised on them since 1999.
grape varieties	100% Chardonnay
production	The more compacted the soil is, the more difficult it is for the roots to penetrate the ground. The root tissues find it difficult to gain sufficient depth to reach the nutrients in the ground. In biodynamic farming, it is therefore important for the soil to be well aerated. This means that the soil is worked solely with horses and carts, encouraging the development of mycorrhiza (a symbiotic association between a fungus and the roots of a host plant). Mycorrhizae feed the grapes, helping to boost their quality. Herbicides, chemical products against false and real mildew, and acaricides (pesticides to combat red spider mite, ticks and other mites) are not used at all. But constant compacting of the soil is not good for the vines either.

→
A piece of
technical
ingenuity for
storing bottles
of the 'Cuvée
des Caudalies'
sur pointe

←
The De Sousa
tasting room

↓
Charlotte
de Sousa listens
intently during
the tasting

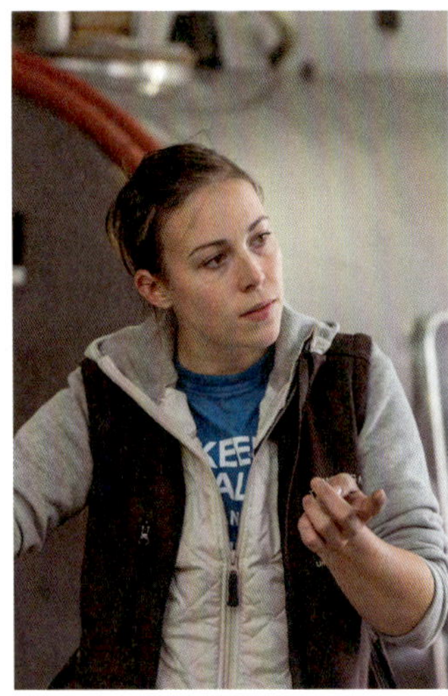

CAUDALIES
Millésime 2008
5.099 /.
EARL DE SOUSA
Tirage 2008 de 14 04 2009
GRAND CRU BLANC DE BLANCS
Cuvée des caudalies MILLÉSIME 2008

Le menu change tous les jours
au gré de l'humeur et des saisons

Menu 39€ Jeudi 16 Juin

L'œuf mollet de ferme
salade d'asperges tiède
à l'anis vert
boudin blanc de Rethel
et crispy de jambon bellotta

La bavette de Bœuf angus
(irlande)
poelée de blé tendre au citron
confit et légumes de saison
au satay

Abricots poelées
Crémeux verveine citron
fruits rouges, sorbet fromage blanc
fromage

CHAMPAGNE DOMAINE JACQUES SELOSSE

A visit to the godfather

Jacques Selosse established the domain in Avize in 1949. He is the father of Anselme who took over the reins in 1974. Anselme studied winegrowing in Beaune, though he was greatly influenced by the Coche-Dury, Lafon and Leflaive wineries.

The house produces 57,000 bottles a year from its 7.5 hectares of vineyards. The Chardonnay plots are on the Côte des Blancs in Cramant, Avize, Le Mesnil-sur-Oger and Oger. The house also owns a few Pinot Noir plots in the Montagne de Reims (in Aÿ, Ambonnay and Mareuil-sur-Aÿ).

Anselme is very grateful to his parents for working hard their whole lives and paying off the banks. This allows him to now make the champagne he wants.

His premises became too small, and in 2008 he went over to take a look at the cellars of the old Bricout-Delbeck champagne house, which closed down in 2003. The cellars were topped by a beautiful country house, and, together with his wife Corinne, he decided to convert it into a hotel-restaurant, 'Les Avisés' – now one of the region's top addresses.

The country house dates back to 1820, when Charles Koch, the heir of a German hotelier family, moved to Avize and established a champagne house. The house has thus been associated with champagne for almost two centuries, and is full of memories. Locally it is known as the 'Château Koch d'Avize'. After complete refurbishment, the hotel-restaurant 'Les Avisés' opened its doors in 2011.

Anselme shows us the splendid view out over the vineyards. The Jacques Selosse domain was one of the first champagne houses I visited. Anselme is a passionate, emotional person, in many ways living in his own world. Because of his maturity and experience, he was known as the godfather of champagne, or sometimes simply as 'Monsieur Champagne'.

Domaine Jacques Selosse

Récoltant manipulant

59, rue de Cramant

F–51190 AVIZE

+ 33 3 26 57 53 56

www.selosse-lesavises.com

→
Anselme Selosse
or Mr Champagne,
the philosopher

→
Anselme Selosse, a
mythical figure among
champagne makers

↓
Anselme lets us taste us
different years and *cuvées*.

Anselme has inspired many young winegrowers in their drive for excellence. He has breathed new life into the art of making wine and has many followers, with many growers adopting his way of making wine.

Anselme Selosse has brought a fresh wind to the region – or perhaps even a revolution – refocusing attention on the wine and not the bubbles. Selosse was also the one focusing attention on the relation between soil health and good wine, challenging traditional ways of making wine and using spontaneous fermentation with a minimum of sulphur. He picks the grapes late and with great care. The wine is stored for at least one year, getting some *bâtonnage* to improve its taste. Malolactic fermentation, according to him, is part of a natural process in the wine's evolution; it allows the vintage effect to be expressed even beyond the picking. Fermentation occurs only in barrels of 228 or 400 litres, of which less than twenty percent are new. The wine stays on the sediments for a long period. 'A great champagne has no need of make-up' is his motto. He is a believer not just in organic winegrowing and low yields, but also in finding the purest expression of the terroir in his champagne.

In 1986, he came up with his so-called 'solera system' for blending of some twenty vintages. While preventing variation between vintages, this promotes the expression of the Avize terroir. He does just the opposite with his millésimés. These always come from the same plot, but have a different taste every year.

No other champagne has met more acclaim than 'Domaine Jacques Selosse' champagne.

In 1994, he was voted France's best winemaker in each category – a unique achievement. The *Revue des Vins de France* awarded him best winemaker of the year in 1993 (for his production) and again in 2016 (for the unstinting support he gave to a new generation of winemakers, both in other regions in France and elsewhere in Europe). His champagnes are thus very much in demand. While we were there, we were lucky to be able to taste the first *mise* of his son Gauthier. It was superb.
The third generation is ready and waiting!

Conclusion

Anselme, the man responsible for putting the wine back into champagne and for restoring the value of the region's best terroirs. Top champagnes, and the next generation is ready and waiting.

Entrance to
the cellars and
the reserve wine
at Selosse

A water lock for the
fermenting wine

→

At Selosse they
are not afraid to
experiment. Here
with amphorae.

←

At Selosse they
ferment only in
wooden barrels

   Champagne Domaine Jacques Selosse

JACQUES
SELOSSE
CHAMPAGNE
APPELLATION CHAMPAGNE CONTRÔLÉE

V.O.
JACQUES SELOSSE
PRODUCE OF FRANCE
750 ml

CUVÉES AND
VINTAGE CHAMPAGNES

A few of his champagnes

BRUT INITIAL, BLANC DE BLANCS

terroir	Plots on the slopes of Cramant, Avize and Oger
grape varieties	100% Chardonnay

ROSÉ

terroir	The Pinot Noir grapes come from Ambonnay.
grape varieties	10% Pinot Noir, 90% Chardonnay

LA CÔTE FARON (FORMERLY CONTRASTE), BLANC DE NOIRS

terroir	Grapes from the La Côte Faron vineyard in Aÿ.
grape varieties	100% Pinot Noir
production	Made using the solera systeem.

LES CARELLES, BLANC DE BLANCS

terroir	The Les Carelles vineyard in Le Mesnil-sur-Oger
grape varieties	100% Chardonnay
type	extra brut
production	Made using the solera systeem.

LE BOUT DU CLOS

classification	grand cru
terroir	The Le Bout du Clos vineyard in Ambonnay
grape varieties	80% Pinot Noir, 20% Chardonnay
type	extra brut
production	Made using the solera systeem.

SOUS LE MONT

classification	grand cru
terroir	The Sous le Mont vineyard in Mareuil-sur-Aÿ
grape varieties	100% Pinot Noir
type	extra brut
production	Made using the solera systeem.

LES CHANTEREINES, BLANC DE BLANCS

terroir	Plots in Avize and Cramant
grape varieties	100% Chardonnay
type	extra brut
production	Made using the solera systeem.

LE CHEMIN DE CHÂLONS, BLANC DE BLANCS

terroir	Plots in Cramant
grape varieties	100% Chardonnay
type	extra brut
production	Made using the solera systeem.

SALON
CUVÉE
1921
BRUT
CHAMPAGNE
ALON
Le Mesnil
Produce of France
SALON
CUVÉE
1925
BRUT
CHAMPAGNE
SALON
Le Mesnil
CUVÉE 1925
Produce of France
SALON
CUVÉE
1928
BRUT
CHAMPAGNE
SALON
Le Mesnil
CUVÉE 1928
Produce of France
MESNIL
SALON
CUVÉE
1953
BRUT
SALON
CUVÉE
1955
BRUT
SALON
CUVÉE
1956
BRUT

CHAMPAGNE SALON

A 'misfit' in Champagne, and a very different story

Although Eugène Aimé Salon was born in the Champagne region in 1867, it did not initially look like he would have anything to do with winegrowing, instead becoming a teacher. But his heart was not in it, and he became a furrier, a trade allowing him to dine every day at Maxim's in Paris. However, he found that the champagne he was served was not to his taste. As he had done quite well out of the fur trade, he decided to start growing wine himself – and not just any wine: his goal right from the beginning was to make a mythical wine: one vintage, one plot, one cru and one grape variety, all from one village, Le Mesnil-sur-Oger.

The grapes for the champagne come from the 1-hectare 'Le Jardin de Salon' and from 19 other plots scattered around Le Mesnil-sur-Oger, all painstakingly selected by Eugène Aimé Salon himself.

The wines were stored on racks in the cellar for at least 10 years, and Salon was no friend of assembly wines, working with 100% Chardonnay.

Champagne Salon

5-7, rue de la Brèche d'Oger

F-51190 LE MESNIL SUR OGER

+ 33 3 26 57 51 65

www.salondelamotte.com

In 1911, he produced his first millésimé from the 1905 vintage, made just for friends and for Maxim's. In 1920, he started marketing his champagne, and it immediately became Maxim's house champagne. This was the first blanc de blancs millésimé and the first *mono-cru* (champagne from grapes from a single vineyard) ever produced.

Dying in 1943, Aimé Salon was succeeded by his nephew. The house Salon remained a family-run business until 1963, and was eventually taken over by the Laurent-Perrier group in 1988, as was its neighbour, the Chardonnay specialist, house Delamotte. The group is today run by Didier Dupond and Michel Fauconnet, Laurent-Perrier's *chef de cave* and production manager.

A number of changes were made. For instance, the oak barrels used for storage were removed, in the hope of preserving the wines' intense *fraîcheur*.

The vines are on average 50 years old. There is no malolactic fermentation and there is only just enough dosage to allow the aromas of the wine to come out. If no Salon is made in any one year, the grapes go to the neighbouring Delamotte house.

Just 37 millésimés were produced in the whole of the 20th century, something that is very unusual. Three millésimés have already been produced in the 21st century, in 2002, 2004 and 2006.

Conclusion   Salon's champagne is unique, always a millésimé Blanc de Blancs, always a *monocépage* of Chardonnay. A top champagne, but not easy to get hold of in the wine trade.

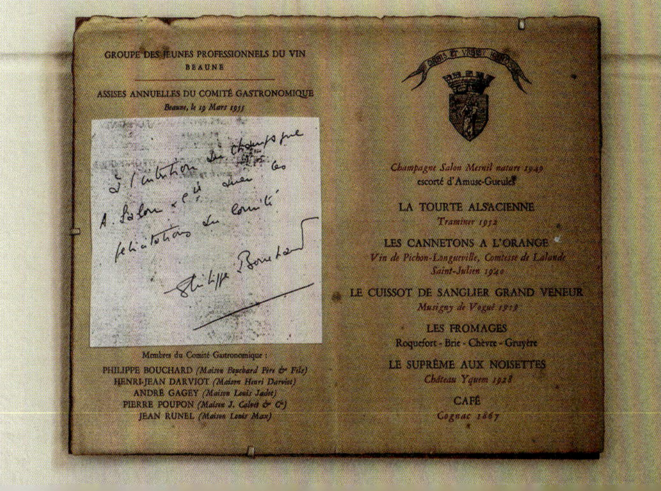

GROUPE DES JEUNES PROFESSIONNELS DU VIN
BEAUNE

ASSISES ANNUELLES DU COMITÉ GASTRONOMIQUE
Beaune, le 19 Mars 1955

Membres du Comité Gastronomique :
PHILIPPE BOUCHARD (Maison Bouchard Père & Fils)
HENRI-JEAN DARVIOT (Maison Henri Darviot)
ANDRÉ GAGEY (Maison Louis Jadot)
PIERRE POUPON (Maison J. Calvet & Cie)
JEAN RUNEL (Maison Louis Max)

Champagne Salon Mesnil nature 1949
escorté d'Amuse-Gueules

LA TOURTE ALSACIENNE
Traminer 1952

LES CANNETONS A L'ORANGE
Vin de Pichon-Longueville, Comtesse de Lalande
Saint-Julien 1940

LE CUISSOT DE SANGLIER GRAND VENEUR
Musigny de Vogüé 1919

LES FROMAGES
Roquefort - Brie - Chèvre - Gruyère

LE SUPRÊME AUX NOISETTES
Château Yquem 1928

CAFÉ
Cognac 1867

CUVÉES AND MILLÉSIMÉS

20TH CENTURY: MILLÉSIMÉS

1905 | Frost in May, storms in June and July, a late harvest during the last 10 days of September.

1909 | Frost in the winter and again in May, rain during the 26 September harvest.

1911 | Early blossom, drought in the summer, harvest on 10-12 September, top weather and perfectly ripe grapes.

1914 | Long period of blossom, mildew in July causing heavy losses, harvest on 28 September.

1921 | Frosts of -7°C to -9°C in April, resulting in an 80% loss; a small but top-quality harvest.

1925 | Hail in spring, great losses, cold nights. Harvesting takes a whole month. Average quality.

1928 | Frost in May, hail, a harvest in the rain, but top quality.

1934 | Frost in May leads to a 6% loss, but the harvest in the middle of September produced top-quality grapes. Superb quality champagne.

1937 | A good year with great discolouration on the berries.

1942 | A cold start to the year, harvest begins on 15 September, grapes with a perfect, exceptional taste. Good quality.

1943 | Quality not so good.

1946 | Slow but irregular blossom. The weather improves before the harvest, which begins by the end of September. Average quality.

1947 | Early harvest, perfect, good-quality grapes.

1948 | Hail in May, July and August. Attaque of botrytis at the end of August, beginning of September. Harvest from 20 September on. You can feel the effect of the botrytis.

1949 | Quick harvest starting on 19 September.

1951 | A catastrophic freeze destroys three-quarters of the vineyards, 70% loss. Late harvest in October. Grapes in a good state but lower quality.

1953 | Healthy grapes, harvest begins on 15 September, lovely weather and quite good quality.

1955 | Frost in May affecting 1,500 hectares in the Marne valley, 400-500 of which are totally destroyed.

1956 | Perfect harvest with good quality.

1959 | Harvest on 10 September, the grapes are perfectly ripe, providing especially good quality.

1961 | Harvest begins on 20 September in perfect weather conditions. Healthy and good-quality grapes.

1964 | Harvest begins with 48 hours of rain. Warm and sunny afterwards, excellent quality.

1966 | The blossom is at its best. Storms from May to August with the loss of 200 hectares. Harvest begins on 26 September in nice weather, delivering great quality grapes for champagne making.

1969 | A series of summer hailstorms lays waste to some 900 hectares. Harvesting begins only on 1 October during a dry and sunny period, helping to give the wine a good quality.

1971 | Hard frost in spring destroys 1,000 hectares. Further 650 hectares hit later by frost, hail and wind. Harvest on 18 September.

1973 | A dry summer, harvest on 28 September, good quality.

1976 | The clusters indicate that there will be a good harvest of grapes. Extremely hot summer, very dry, the grapes begin to change colour early in August. That is unusually early and many winegrowers have to return from their holidays to pick the grapes. Just 84 days between blossom and harvest. This delivers perfect grapes with a high sugar level, good ripeness and low acidity, giving a strong and subtle champagne with a good taste of wine.

1979 | Harvest from 3 to 8 October, healthy grapes give a nice, aromatic wine.

1982 | Fantastic conditions, harvest begins on 17 and 20 September. The house had harvested nothing during the last two years.

1983 | Exceptional year. Following a bad spring, the grapes are harvested on 28 September. Very unusual to get two good years in a row. The last time this happened was in 1928-29.

1985 | A very hard winter, with temperatures down to –25°C.
The roots stop growing and a number of vines have to be
taken out. Great weather for ripening the grapes from
July onwards. The harvest begins on 20 September,
following a year of extremes.

1988 | It looked like a perfunctory year, but following the
harvest on September 26 we can speak of one of the most
remarkable champagnes ever made. This is the year
with the greatest expression.

1990 | A bad start to the year with frost on 5 April and
a second dose of freezing cold beginning on 19 April.
Some 45% of the vineyards were hit. After lots of bad
weather, the summer turns out to be very dry.
Harvesting the exceptional grapes begins on 14 September.
Another top.

1995 | A mild year without surprises, sunny spring,
warm summer. The harvest begins on 23 September.
Delicious champagne.

1996 | One of Salon's best years. Warm spring, exceptional
sugar levels. Top.

1997 | The third good year in a row. Harvest on 22 September
following a hot summer.

1999 | A relatively mild winter, with a few (hail)storms.
The second last year of the 20th century is the hottest
of the century, delivering the largest harvest ever.

21ST CENTURY: MILLÉSIMÉS

2002 | What a great year! A perfect combination of fresh and soft,
rain and drought. No freezing cold, no hail. The vines are
in a top condition. No risk for the vineyard. Harvesting
takes place on 16 September in splendid weather.

2004 | The grapes ripen late and are thinned out. The sun
appears on 2 September and let the grapes mature until
harvest on 27 September. Good acidity. We can speak of
a top millésimé.

2006 | Ideal weather conditions. Not too many, not too few
grapes. A top year.

CHAMPAGNE JACQUESSON

The Jacquesson champagne house is a *négociant-manipulant* and produces 250,000 bottles a year. The house was founded in 1798 by Claude Jacquesson. The family name remained alive because Claude's grandson Adolphe invented the *muselet*, the wire hood that is stretched around the cork. Before that, the cork was held fast with string, but would sometimes come loose in transport.

Napoleon Bonaparte visited the Jacquesson cellars and was immediately convinced of the quality. The imperial gold medal that he presented to the house in 1810 made it much more widely known.

Fifty years later, the Jacquessons sold the estate to the Tassigny family, which made the house a great name in the 1920s. Under the name of B.B., it produced a blanc de blancs that was popular with members of parliament. Tassigny bought the attractive vineyards in Oizy, Avize, Hautvillers and Dizy, but those first glory years were never matched again. Since 1867, Jacquesson has already sold a million bottles.

In 1974, the Jacquesson house was sold to Jacques Chiquet. Jacques' sons, Laurent and Jean-Hervé, are still in charge today. Laurent is responsible for production, Jean-Hervé for sales and management of the domain.

Négociant manipulant
250,000 bottles

Champagne Jacquesson
68, rue du Colonel Fabien
F–51530 DIZY
+ 33 3 26 55 68 11
www.champagnejacquesson.com

Today, their vineyards are spread over two different regions: the Côte des Blancs region in the villages of Avize and Oizy with only grand crus, and the Vallée de la Marne region with a grand cru in Aÿ and two premier crus in the villages of Dizy and Hautvillers. The vineyards on the Côte des Blancs are completely south facing, while those in the Vallée de la Marne face east, south and southwest and have a chalk substrate.

↑
Jean-Hervé
Chiquet, the
visionary among
the champagne
makers

We made an appointment with Jean-Hervé. He walked us around and told us the details of the house. '80% of the grapes come from our own vineyards, 20% we buy from neighbours. We always buy in a small amount of grapes to manage the domain. These grapes come from adjacent plots, so we can always keep an eye on the state of the vineyard. In addition, we can have these grapes delivered directly to our press.'

For the Chiquet brothers it is important that their vineyards, like most premiers and grands crus, lie above a several hundred metres thick chalk pillar, but also enjoy a very special semi-continental climate where the average temperature never goes above 10°C.

The Chiquets work traditionally, usually with short pruning, and as biologically as possible. 'We especially want to place a brake on the natural strength of the vineyard to better reflect the properties of each plot and to allow the influence of the mineral to dominate the fruit. We're not interested in a high return.' The brothers also want to show that the work of humans in the vineyard is very important. *'Le terroir, même grand, n'est rien sans le travail de l'homme'* (A terroir, however large, is nothing without the work of man). Most premiers and grands crus from Champagne lie above the 49th latitude, and at this latitude, it is certainly not a problem to have enough acidity. This is very important for the champagne house.

The white wine comes mainly from blue grapes, so they have to be very careful during maceration and pigmentation to prevent colouring juice. The same attention is paid to the pips and the stalks: given the location, they never reach the same ripeness as in regions further south. It is important that they remain intact to prevent unwanted tannin and bitterness from sneaking into the wine. For this reason, the house uses a vertical press, the juice from which is less coloured and less rich in tannin.

↗
Here the pressed
grapes are turned
over for producing
the *vin de presse*

↓
A 19th century
advertisement

It is not filtered or clarified: the latter process happens naturally. The second juice from the pressing is not used and is systematically resold. 'Sometimes we even sell all our juice. If we find that the quality is insufficient, we sell the juice rather than keep it as a *vin de réserve*'. They work with gravity and never add sugar. For the vinification they use oak, because they believe that oak is the only material that allows the wine to breath. This takes place either in old *foudres* or in 500 litre *demi-muids*.

The wines need to rest for four to five months *sur lies* and undergo *bâtonnage*. Cold stabilization is not used.

We ask where the strange name *Cuvée 700* comes from. 'It's the only assembly champagne we make, and it looks different every year. This cuvée has a different profile each year. We consciously do not call this champagne a *brut sans année* because this would require us to offer always a consistent quality. To us, only outstanding quality is important, and so we came up with the idea of giving this cuvée a number. We chose the production number of the cuvée, like the ones we use to record the different bottlings in our books. Cuvée number 1 was given that number in 1898 when the  first centenary of the champagne house was celebrated. In 2000 we started the series Cuvées 700 with number 728. The intention is also that the cuvée not fall under the shadow of the *lieux-dits* (parts of the vineyard).'

The house has four more *lieux-dits* that their father bought. Jean-Hervé: 'However, in 1988 we started to change the working methods. The Cuvée 700 was a nice transition to the *lieux-dits*.'

When we say that the Jacquesson champagne had a light oxidative touch in the 2000s, Jean-Hervé does not completely deny it. Most of the people who know the champagne say therefore that Jacquesson champagne expresses the taste of the Chiquet brothers, and for Jean-Hervé, this is true.

Conclusion   Jacquesson is the phoenix of boutique champagnes.

CUVÉES AND MILLÉSIMÉS

ARCHIVES CUVÉES

Cuvée 700

assembly	different years
type	brut
production	Only the first pressing is used. The wine is vinified in *foudres* and not filtered.
results	The first cuvée dates from 2000. The champagne has good ageing potential. The following numbers are already available: 728, 729,730, 731, 732, 733DT, 734DT, 735, 736, 737, 738 and 739.

Dizy Corne Bautray

terroir	The vineyard is located in Dizy on high, steep south-west-facing slopes. The vineyard is one hectare in size and has been planted with 9,000 Chardonnay vines since 1960. The chablis pruning method is used.
soil	clay, stone and chalk
grape varieties	Chardonnay
results	annual production of 5,000 bottles

Dizy Terres Rouges

terroir	The vineyards are at the bottom of the slope and face eastwards.
soil	brown-red limestone soil
results	annual production of about 9,000 bottles

Avize Champ Caïn 2002-2004-2005

terroir	The vineyards are at the bottom of the slopes and face southwards. The vineyards consist of about 12,000 vines planted in 1962 on 1.5 hectares. The chablis pruning method is used.
soil	lime, clay, sand, limestone and chalk pebbles
production	The wines are stored *sur lies* for eight years before *dégorgement*.

Aÿ Vauzelle Terme

terroir	located halfway up steep, south-facing slopes. There are 2,500 Pinot Noir vines on 30 ares. The vines were planted in 1980. The 'Cordon De Royan pruning method is used.
soil	lime on chalk
grape varieties	Pinot Noir
results	annual production of about 2,000 bottles.

MILLÉSIMÉS

1988DT, 1989DT, 1990DT, 1995DT, 1996, 1997, 2000, 2002

assembly	millésime
production	DT means *'dégorgement tardif'* or ' late disgorgement'. That is, the champagnes ripen on racks for longer.

→
Old oak foudres or demi-muids. Oak is the only material that allows wine to breathe.

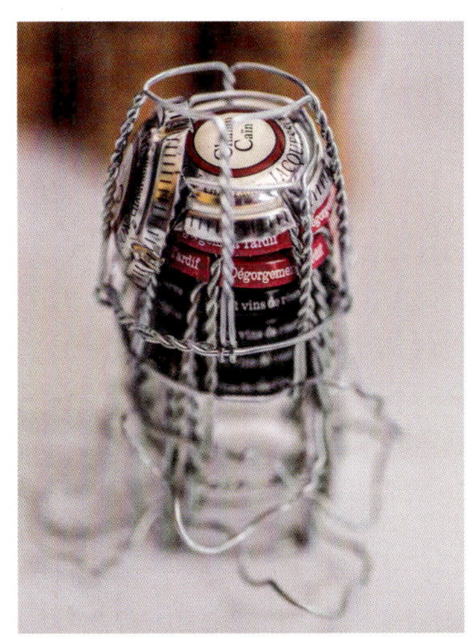

CHAMPAGNE FALLET-PRÉVOSTAT

A well-kept treasure

At the heart of Avize, we went looking for the champagne house Fallet-Prévostat. In fact, we walked past it several times, as there is not even a nameplate on the big gate. When it does open, a resolute old woman, Madame Fallet, stands in front us.

The house is media-shy and the proprietor asks us not to take too many pictures, 'we do not like advertising; we also have no sales representative. We sell our champagne only here in the house.' In her kitchen, time has stood still: a beautiful faded flower wallpaper, a floral oilcloth on the table, a typical 1950s interior.

Gradually she thaws and tells her story: as the daughter of a winegrower, she attended the technical school and on obtaining her diploma went to work with the village notary. She met her husband, a winegrower like her father. When her daughters were born, she quit her job and began working full time with her husband. Together they own 4.7 hectares in Avize – the Côtes des Blancs, all grand cru, and produce an average of 28,000 bottles a year. It's hard work and every minute of free time is spent in the vineyards.

They work almost entirely alone and have a very personal approach. Monsieur and madame are both in their eighties, which raises the question of whether there are successors in the family. The two daughters have become doctors, and lack both the time and inclination to take over the domain. There was talk of grandson Thomas, a history student, coming into the business, but unfortunately, to madame's regret, that did not happen.

'As long as our health allows, we will continue to work', she says proudly.

**Champagne
Fallet-Prévostat**

56, rue Pasteur

F–51190 AVIZE

+ 33 3 26 57 51 97

We are invited to visit the cellars. They consist of underground corridors dating from the 18th century, two floors below street level. The corridors are packed with bottles, stacked up to the ceiling. A corpulent person would struggle to pass through.

What strikes us is that the champagne is stored for seven years *sur lattes*. The idea is to have sufficient reserves in the event of a setback, like a disastrous harvest. However, even when champagne was not fashionable, they had noticed that a nice ageing benefited the taste of the wine.

They had their first cuvée in 1957 and three years later, in 1960, they brought it onto the market.

In total they have three cuvées, all 100% Chardonnay.

The cellars at Fallet-Prévostat, two floors below street level, with unique view of the rail system in the crowded cellar

CUVÉES AND MILLÉSIMÉS

Cuvée Prestige

classification	grand cru
grape varieties	100% Chardonnay

Prévostat extra brut

classification	grand cru
grape varieties	100% Chardonnay
type	extra brut

Prévostat brut

classification	grand cru
grape varieties	100% Chardonnay
type	brut

CHAMPAGNE ÉGLY-OURIET

**'Les vignes c'est comme les chevaux,
si tu veux bien les maîtriser,
il faut les faire naître.'
(Vines are like horses, to master them you must first breed them.)**

Shortly after the Second World War, Charles Égly founded the Égly-Ouriet house
with his wife Andrée Ouriet in Ambonnay. They grew grapes, which they sold to
the big houses. Very gradually, they started making their own champagne. They
were among the first to switch to the *récoltant-manipulant* system. We had made an

appointment with their grandson, Francis Égly. Égly-Ouriet is not a
big house, producing on average only 100,000 bottles a year, but the
wines are of high quality. In total, they have 12 hectares, of which
9.7 ha Grand Cru, mostly in Ambonnay (7.7 ha) and in Bouzy and
Verzenay. These vineyards are all in the grand cru region. The two
hectares of premier cru are at Vrigny in the Marne valley.

On taking over the estate from his father Michel in 1980, Francis
had a clear plan: he wanted to bring the Pinot Noir grape to the
absolute top and to work in the best possible
way. He started by lowering the yield, and by
using only the first juice from the pressing. He
worked his vineyards according to biodynamic
principles, at a time when this was not yet in.

He used spontaneous fermentation and vinified in oak barrels.
To maintain freshness, there is no malolactic fermentation and
the wine remains at least three years *sur lattes*. For Francis, it is
not only the perfect quality of the grapes that gives a beautiful
structure and complexity to their champagnes. 'We also pay a lot
of attention and care in the basement to allow the wine to age
nicely and long on its lees. We are very particular and precise,
both in the vineyard and in the cellar. Certain cuvées are kept for
four years *sur lies* and some of our cuvées as long as 112 months.
In this way the terroir is very pronounced in the glass.'

Champagne Égly-Ouriet

15, rue de Trépail

F–51150 AMBONNAY

+ 33 3 26 57 00 70

The average age of the vines here is thirty-five years, for the cuvées prestiges it is sixty years. The Blanc de Noirs V.V. (*Vieilles Vignes*) is made of grapes from seventy-year-old vines.

Almost all cuvées approach perfection. 'Our champagnes are powerful champagnes in their own category. They are rich and complex', says Francis. Many of the champagnes are extra brut and with a fine *dosage*. Given their success, each importer receives only a limited number of bottles.

According to Francis, real champagne has been made only since the Second World War.

What is important is the work in the vineyard, the pressing and time, lots of time. For Francis, champagne is especially the art of pressing the grapes in different stages. For this, you must know your grapes and pips.

Proud, confident but not arrogant, and rational, he stands in front of his *coquard à plateau incliné*, a modern coquard press that presses sideways. New is the chilled tank, which collects the juice and immediately cools it. The advantage is that you have better control.

We visit Francis at the nervous start of the 2017 harvest. Everything is spick and span and Francis does not quit the press because the grapes are coming. The basement and pressing room are tidy and incredibly clean, with zero margin for error. In the vineyard, Francis tells us that the family are horse riders. I ask whether he also works the vineyards with horses, but no, he does not believe in that. He works in the vineyard with light equipment.

He thinks he will probably not make a millésimé in 2017. Nature has played too many tricks on him this year.

Conclusion   What Anselme Selosse is in Avize, Francis Égly is in Ambonnay: an icon.

→
The grand cru vineyard at Ambonnay. Francis Égly meticulously follows the entire wine-making process from start to finish.

↓
Francis Égly, the icon of Ambonnay

CHAMPAGNE EGLY O
AMBONNAY

D 26
AMBONNAY

CUVÉES AND MILLÉSIMÉS

Égly-Ouriet Les Vignes de Vrigny

classification	premier cru
terroir	Vrigny
grape varieties	100% Pinot Meunier
production	stored in stainless steel vats, 3 years *sur lies*

Égly-Ouriet brut tradition grand cru

classification	grand cru
terroir	90% of the grapes are from the grand cru village of Ambonnay, 10% from the grand cru villages of Verzenay and Bouzy
grape varieties	70% Pinot Noir, 30% Chardonnay
type	brut
production	48 months *sur lies*, vinification in barrels

Égly-Ouriet brut rosé grand cru

classification	grand cru
terroir	The grapes are from Ambonnay (almost all Chardonnay, 5% Pinot Noir), Verzenay and Bouzy
grape varieties	80% Pinot Noir, 20% Chardonnay
production	48 months *sur lies*, vinification in barrels

Égly-Ouriet grand cru 2007 millésimé

classification	grand cru
terroir	100% grand cru from Ambonnay
grape varieties	70% Pinot Noir, 30% Chardonnay
assembly	millésime
production	96 months *sur lies*, vinification in barrels

Égly-Ouriet V.P. extra brut

classification	grand cru
terroir	90% of the grapes are from the grand cru village of Ambonnay, 10% from the grand cru villages of Verzenay and Bouzy.
grape varieties	70% Pinot Noir, 30% Chardonnay
type	extra brut
production	84 months *sur lies*, vinification in barrels. V.P. stands for *Vieillissement prolongé* (extended ageing).

Égly-Ouriet Blanc de Noirs V.V.

classification	grand cru
terroir	vineyard 'Les Crayères'
soil	30 centimetres of topsoil, the rest is limestone.
grape varieties	100% Pinot Noir
production	V.V. stands for *Vieilles Vignes* (old vines). Vinified in wood, 70 months *sur lies*, vinification in barrels

Égly-Ouriet Ambonnay rouge 2013

terroir	from the Coteaux Champenois. All grapes come from a single plot with old vines.
grape varieties	100% Pinot Noir
production	This is a still wine made from the best years.

EGLY-OURIET

www.lannoo.com
Register on our website and we will send you a regular newsletter
with information about new books and interesting, exclusive offers.

Text: Pieter Verheyde
Photography: Andrew Verschetze
English translation: Michael, Richard and Mathieu Lomax
Graphic design: Steven Theunis, Armée de verre

If you have comments or questions,
please contact our editorial team at:
redactielifestyle@lannoo.com

© Uitgeverij Lannoo nv, Tielt, 2018
D/2018/45/126 – NUR 440-447
ISBN 978 94 014 3475 1

All rights reserved. No part of this edition may be reproduced,
stored in an automated retrieval system and/or be published in any form
or by any means, electronic, mechanical or other, without
the prior written permission of the publisher.